A
Taste of the

British
Virgin Islands

A

Step-by-Step Cookbook

By

Angela Spenceley

A Taste of the British Virgin Island
A Step-by-Step Cookbook

By Angela Spenceley

Dedicated to Lumi, my assistant and best friend, who stood by me during a tough time.

Published by:
Coconut Press, LLC
P.O. Box 79710,
Carolina, PR 00984-9710
www.coconut-press.com

ISBN 0-9778913-3-X

Printed in India

For additional copies or bulk sales, contact Coconut Press.
First Edition Published 2007

Contents

Introduction

*T*he British Virgin Islands are the islands you dream of being shipwrecked on...Close your eyes and dream of an aquamarine Caribbean Sea the temperature of bath water, palms rustled by tradewinds, coconuts thunking on powdery, white sand-these are the islands Christopher Columbus sighted on his second voyage in 1493.

The Virgin Islands, named by Columbus for St. Ursula and her 11,000 virgins, are a network of 90 small islands, cays (pronounced "keys") and islets in the Eastern Caribbean, about 40 miles east of Fajardo, Puerto Rico. By jet, the islands are two and a half hours from Miami, or 1,100 miles south of this Floridian city, and 1,500 miles south of New York.

The Atlantic Ocean washes the northern shore of the islands, the Caribbean Sea, to the south. The islands spread out over 195 square miles, and comprise two groups: the British Virgin Islands and the U.S. Virgin Islands. The U.S. islands are considerably more commercialized with bustling tourism and inner commerce, while the British islands have retained their laid back, unspoiled beauty.

The British Virgin Islands consist of four main islands: Tortola, Virgin Gorda, Anegada, and Jost Van Dyke, along with 32 smaller islands, including pristine Peter Island (across the bay from Road Town Harbor on Tortola). Most of the islands, except Anegada, a coral island with lagoons, salt ponds and miles of gorgeous beaches, are volcanic in origin, heaved up from the sea bed. The rock is sedimentary, and the water depth is about 165 feet, dropping to 2,580 fathoms in the St. Croix Deep trench.

Sixteen of the 36 British Virgin Islands are inhabited. Tortola, the most lively, covers 21 square miles and is the seat of the capital, Road Town. Tortola is mountainous, with few wide open spaces and flat areas. Mount Sage, 1,780 feet, is the highest point in both the U.S. and British Virgin Islands.

Anegada spreads over 15 square miles and is no more than 20 feet above sea level. Smaller, yet gorgeous, Virgin Gorda, covers 8 square miles, its highest area is Gorda Peak at 1,370 feet. Virgin Gorda boasts an unusual geological formation known as The Baths. House-size boulders strewn along a waterside area south of Spanish Town form a maze of sunlit grottoes and caves. Hilly, but with miles of sandy beaches, diminutive Jost Van Dyke has an area of only 3 square miles.

What's unique about the British Virgin Islands is their diversity: rolling hills, steep mountainsides with breathtaking ocean views, gently rolling plains, coral reefs and lagoons to stretches of palm-rimmed, white sand beaches.

The U.S. and British Virgin Islands are divided by Drake's Passage, a channel named after privateer Sir Francis Drakes. Queen Elisabeth of England gave Drake command of a fleet of 25 ships, and free reign to plunder as many Spanish treasure ships as possible. Occasionally, Drake operated outside the law, venturing into outright piracy.

Dutch pirates established the first major settlement on the West End of Tortola in 1648. Thanks to prodding by the pirates, farmers introduced livestock such as cattle and pigs to the area, which greatly increased commerce in ships looking to trade spices, grain and other luxuries for meat. Sugarcane cultivation also took root.

In the 1660's the British kicked the Dutch out, and have taken over ever since. However, for nearly 150 years, the islands were the haunts of infamous pirates such as Blackbeard, Calico Jack Rackham, and his wench, Anne Bonny, Captain Kidd, and Henry Avery. In the 17th and 18th century, cotton, then sugar cane was introduced, and the islands prospered, until slavery was abolished in 1834. The islands declined, and in 1900 the population was just 5000. In 1960, the British Virgin Islands became a Crown Colony of Britain presided over by a Governor, appointed by the British Monarch.

Both the U.S. and British Virgin Islands enjoy ideal weather: sunshine 365 days a year, cooled by tradewinds, which keeps the humidity at bay. Temperatures range between 70°F and 90°F.

Tourism accounts for half the island's income, with offshore banking running a close second with its 150,000 registered banking and financial companies. There is a small fishing industry, as well as boat building, and rum distillation. Agriculture still plays a role, with the islands having a wide variety of habitats from beach coastline, mangroves, desert and mountain areas. Flowering plants include hibiscus, bougainvillea, jasmine, heliconia, bromeliads, orchids and many more tropical beauties.

Many of the trees are grown for food and spices: avocado, coconut, mango, fig, guava, banana, plantain, limes, papaya, passionfruit, cinnamon, nutmeg, cocoa, and breadfruit.

Four distinctly different cultures have influenced cuisine in the islands: Amerindians (Carib and Arawaks from South America); European; African and Asian. The Amerindians grew corn, cassava, beans, sweet potatoes, garlic, tobacco and peppers. Pineapple, guava, papaya, cashews and the occasional fish and wild pigeon supplemented the Indians diet. The Arawaks are thought to be the originators of grinding cassava, draining the poisonous juice in order to make flour for bread.

The next group, European, comprises four sub-groups with each island(s) dominated by its colorful heritage: the Hispanic influencing Puerto Rico, the Dominican Republic and Cuba. When Columbus and his men arrived in the Caribbean, they found the available food of the Amerindians to be rather limited. Flour, oil, vinegar, as well as livestock, pigs and cows were dispatched from Spain. Later, the French, shaped cuisine in Haiti, St. Martin, Guadeloupe, St. Barths, and Martinique; the British did the same for the British Virgin Islands, Jamaica, Barbados, Grenada; and the Dutch subsequently for St. Maarten, Aruba and Curaçao.

With the importation of African slaves to work the sugar plantations, a number of new foods and cooking methods were introduced. The slaves, highly bored with the little bits of meat and fish served to them by the plantation owners, decided to spice things up a bit. They brought yams, pigeon peas, beans, okra, ackee, and taro. Rich thick stews were seasoned with scallions, parsley, coriander and thyme.

Slavery was abolished by 1838, and all the Africans left the vast plantations. Freed slaves from other islands and indentured servants from India and China filled the huge deficit in labor. The Asians introduced their own spices, cooking methods and utensils. East Indian curries, rice, spices, yogurt and ghee (clarified butter) were added to the Caribbean menu.

All of the Caribbean islands are in close proximity to each other. Eventually Spanish, French, Dutch, African and Asian cuisine made its way to the British Virgin Islands. In the BVI, you'll find many unusual dishes. **Jerk** was brought to the islands by the Arawak Indians, and is a way of curing meat rubbed in spices and cooked over a slow fire. The spices included fiery, habañero peppers, allspice, cinnamon, nutmeg, thyme, brown sugar and other condiments. **Conch** (pronounced konk) is the muscle of the conch shell, and found plentifully all over the islands and incorporated in everything from ravioli, conch chowder to conch fritters. **Fungi** sounds awful, but they're really dumplings made from okra and cornmeal. Other side dishes often served include: **plantain, yams, sweet potatoes, rice and pigeon peas.** You'll still find **saltfish** (old-style way of preserving cod fish with salt) and **patés** (flaky pastries filled with spiced beef, chicken or fish), and **rotis,** another sort of rolled pastry filled with vegetables, seafood, chicken, conch or meat.

In the British Virgin Islands, you'll find a huge variety of choices when it comes to eating out, from old-time island cuisine, such as the Roti Palace in Tortola to the exquisite, island-inspired menu at the Sugar Mill Hotel. In the pages of this cookbook, I've condensed the British Virgin Island gastronomical experience-from traditional Conch Chowder, to Caribbean fusion Grilled Yellowtail Snapper with Black Bean, Mango and Coconut Salsa to decadent Chocolate Rum Cake.

The recipes in this cookbook are basic and simple, with easy-to-find ingredients. Perfect for Sunday afternoon experimenting. Enjoy!

Appetizers, Soups & Salads
Stamp & Go
MAKES 24

8 ounces salt cod fish, pre-soaked in hot water for 24 hours
1 cup all-purpose flour
1 teaspoon sugar
1¾ teaspoons baking powder
¼ teaspoon baking soda
½ teaspoon freshly cracked black pepper
½ teaspoon salt

¼ teaspoon ground cumin
1 large egg, lightly beaten
¼ cup evaporated milk
1 medium onion, minced
½ small green bell pepper, minced
2 garlic cloves, crushed
½ small habañero pepper, seeded and minced
vegetable oil for frying

1. Drain fish, rinse under cool running water, and squeeze out excess water. Place in large saucepan. Cover fish with water; bring to boil over medium heat, lower heat and cover. Simmer for 15 minutes.

2. Drain fish again, reserving water. Pick out any bones or skin, and discard. Flake fish with a fork and set aside.

3. Sift flour, sugar, baking powder, baking soda, black pepper, salt and cumin into a large bowl.

4. Combine egg, milk and ¼ cup of reserved cooking water in another bowl. Stir into flour mixture. You should have a stiff batter.

5. Incorporate fish, onion, green pepper, garlic, and habañero pepper into batter.

6. Heat 2 inches of vegetable oil in a deep skillet or fryer to 350° F. Drop batter by tablespoonfuls into fat, frying until golden. Drain on food-grade white paper towels.

Coconut Shrimp
SERVES 4

No good Caribbean cookbook would be complete without a recipe for Coconut Shrimp. There are literally hundreds of species of coconut trees growing in the islands. They grow prolifically in the Caribbean's tropical climate. Coconuts have a tendency to drop at inopportune times. Hence, you'll see hotel gardeners pruning coconut trees regularly.

24 large raw shrimp, deveined, shelled, tails on
1 cup unsweetened coconut milk
¼ cup cream of coconut (Coco Lopez™)
¾ cup all-purpose flour
1 teaspoon salt

1 teaspoon freshly cracked black pepper
1 cup fresh grated coconut (see sidebar), or 1 cup unsweetened, shredded
vegetable oil for frying

1. Rinse shrimp under cool running water. Pat dry. Combine coconut milk and cream of coconut in a small dish large enough to dip shrimp. Combine flour, salt and pepper in another small dish; the same for grated coconut.

2. Dip shrimp in coconut milk mixture, then in flour, again in coconut milk. Roll in shredded coconut flakes.

3. Heat 1-inch of vegetable oil with a high smoke point, such as peanut, corn or hazelnut oil.

4. Fry shrimp until golden on all sides, careful not to crowd pan as this will lower temperature of oil and cause shrimp to absorb too much oil.

5. Drain on food-grade paper towels. (specifically marked microwave as paper towels can contain formaldehyde for strengthening). Serve with Mango-Chutney (see index) or Spicy Mango Mustard Sauce.

Spicy Mango Mustard Sauce

MAKES 1 ¾ CUPS

You can substitute peach or apricot preserves for the mango preserves.

1 cup mango preserves
½ cup Dijon-style mustard

¼ habañero or jalapeño pepper, seeded and minced

Combine all ingredients in a small bowl. Serve with fritters, fried shrimp or fried vegetables.

How to Crack and Grate Fresh Coconut

Fresh coconut meat is delicious and superior in recipes to dried. First, look for coconuts without mold. Check the eyes, and be on the lookout for cracks. Choose coconuts that are heavy for their size.

Heat oven to 400° F. Hammer through one of the eyes using a clean nail. Drain liquid and reserve for drinks and cooking. Bake coconut 15 minutes. Use a hammer to crack shell, and pry out meat with a sharp knife. Remove brown inside skin with a vegetable peeler.

Grate by hand or run through a food processor.

West Indian Conch Fritters with Fiery Cocktail Sauce

MAKES 20 TO 25 FRITTERS

Conch fritters figure prominently throughout the Caribbean and the Florida Keys. These tiny fried croquettes of ground conch, breadcrumbs, herbs and vegetables can be found as far south as Aruba. Since they freeze well, double the recipe, and reheat for spur of the moment guests. This fritter recipe has a firm texture, nice for a light lunch. Serve with a green side salad, and ice-cold beer.

1¼ **pounds conch, cleaned (see sidebar) and run through a food processor**
8 **ounces plain breadcrumbs**
3 **small eggs, lightly beaten**
1 **small rib celery, minced**
1 **red bell pepper, minced**
1 **medium yellow onion, minced**
2 **tablespoons fresh minced parsley, preferably flat-leafed; or 1 tablespoon dried**
1 **teaspoon minced fresh thyme; or ½ teaspoon dried**

2 **tablespoons cider vinegar**
3 **tablespoons water**
½ **teaspoon fresh lime zest**
½ **teaspoon salt**
½ **teaspoon freshly cracked black pepper**
3 **tablespoons Tabasco™**
¾ **cup crushed Saltine™ crackers vegetable oil for frying**

1. Place conch, breadcrumbs, eggs, celery, pepper, onion, parsley, thyme, vinegar, water, lime zest, salt, pepper and Tabasco© in food processor. Grind until well combined, and then transfer to a large bowl.

2. Heat oil in a deep skillet over medium-high heat to 350°.

3. Wet hands, scoop up golf-ball sized balls and flatten slightly. Roll in crushed crackers. Fry fritters 3 at a time (do not over load skillet, as this will reduce heat of oil, causing the fritters to become greasy), 4 to 5 minutes on each side, or until golden.

4. Drain on white paper towels. Serve with cocktail sauce. Note: do not use printed paper towels. I prefer to use the kind indicated for food usage, such as the kind that specify microwave safe.

Fiery Cocktail Sauce

MAKES 1 ½ CUPS

This relatively simple sauce can be upgraded, by grating your own fresh horseradish. The capers add an interesting tang.

- 1 cup catsup
- 2 tablespoons grated horseradish
- ½ small habañero pepper, carefully seeded and minced
- 1 tablespoons capers, minced
- 2 tablespoons fresh Key Lime or lime juice
- 1 tablespoon Worcestershire™ sauce
- 1 teaspoon Tabasco™
- ½ teaspoon freshly cracked black pepper

1. Combine catsup, horseradish, habañero, capers, lime juice, Worcestershire™, Tabasco™ and black pepper in a small bowl.

2. Cover and refrigerate until thoroughly chilled. Serve with conch fritters.

Conch

Conch, pronounced 'konk', is a spiral-shaped gastropod, resembling a giant snail found off the coasts of Florida, Gulf coasts and the Caribbean. Conch is tough and requires tenderizing before use. It can be eaten raw, like a salad, if marinated. West coast cooks may substitute abalone for conch.

*Purchase: Conch can be purchased in the shell, or if you're lucky enough to find it, frozen, whole or ground in some gourmet grocers.

*Removing from shell: Here are few popular methods I found: **A:** Place in freezer for 48 hours, remove and thaw in cold water until thawed, conch can then be readily removed; or **B:** Scrub outer shell under cold, running water, place in a deep kettle, cover with water, bring to boil, adding a tablespoon of salt and 1/3 cup of fresh lemon juice. Boil for 3 to 4 minutes. When conch has gone back into its shell, remove from boiling water, then drain in a metal colander (plastic will melt from the heat) under cool running water. Conch can then be removed from shell with a long strong fork, such as the kind used for barbequing; or **C:** Place conch on a large, heavy wood cutting board, opening side down. At the top of the spiral, measure down about 2 inches, and puncture using an ice pick and a hammer. Jam ice pick inside, and twist to get the conch free. Pick up shell, open side down, and conch will fall out. Pry with ice pick if needed.

To clean: Not all of the conch muscle is edible. Using a sharp knife, slice off the orange mantle, eyes and darker area adjacent to foot. Devein, then make vertical scores through skin, and peel off outer membrane. Rinse under cool running water.

To Tenderize: The meat from these large snails is extremely tough. I remember having conch chowder as a teenager on Back Street in St. Thomas in the U.S. Virgin Islands. Tomato-based, fragrant and spicy, inevitably there would be just one chewy piece of conch not minced small enough. **A:** The conch purchased in gourmet stores is usually sold tenderized, so no further treatment is needed. **B:** Conch may be run through a food grinder or food processor. No tenderizing necessary then. **C:** Pound with a mallet to break up the tough tendons. **D:** Slice conch thinly, place in kettle, cover with cold water and bring to boil. Reduce heat at once, and simmer for 1 and a half to 2 hours. Soak conch in vinegar or lime juice for 1 hour. Rinse then place in pressure cooker. Cover with

Pick Up Salt Fish

SERVES 6

'My ex-husband's grandmother (originally from Tortola in the British Virgin Islands) served this at family parties. The longer you soak the salt fish, the less salty it will be. Excess salt consumption leaches calcium from your bones.

2	pounds salt fish	5	cloves garlic, crushed
1	green bell pepper, seeded, and cut in thin strips	1	tablespoons freshly shredded parsley
1	red bell pepper, seeded, and cut in thin strips	½	cup olive oil
		¼	cup apple-cider vinegar
1	medium onion, thinly sliced	1	teaspoon freshly cracked black pepper
1	stalk celery, diced		
½	small habañero pepper, seeded and minced	½	teaspoon dried thyme
		½	teaspoon dried oregano
		¼	teaspoon dried dill

1. Place fish in a large bowl and fill with cool water. Soak overnight in refrigerator. Drain, rinse and fill bowl again. Soak for two hours in the refrigerator. Drain, rinse, repeat. Flake salt fish, removing any bones, and press out as much water as possible.

2. Combine bell peppers, onion, celery, habañero pepper, garlic, parsley, olive oil, vinegar, black pepper, thyme, oregano and dill in a large bowl.

3. Flake in salt fish and toss gently to combine. Refrigerate for at least several hours to marinate. Traditionally served with hard-boiled eggs, toast or crackers.

Salt Island

This island gets its name from the natives who made their living by collecting salt from the lagoons, drying it, and selling to passing ships. Rent for the island used to be one sack of salt a year. Population is just a handful of people now. The island's claim to fame is the wreck of the Royal mail ship, the **RMS Rhone,** anchored off Peter Island when a hurricane hit in 1867. The ship was ripped from her anchor, and driven on the rocks off Salt Island. The site is now a Marine National Park. Even if you don't dive, you can still see the vessel through the clear water.

Herring Gundy

SERVES 6 TO 8

Herring Gundy is a Danish dish, traditionally served on Good Fridays in the U.S. and British Virgin Islands. You can substitute lobster, shrimp, any firm white fish, salt cod fish, fresh or canned salmon or tuna.

2	pounds smoked herring	1	celery stalk, diced
1	large onion, thinly sliced	3	tablespoons shredded parsley
1	green bell pepper, seeded and thinly sliced in strips	¼	cup apple-cider vinegar
1	red bell pepper, seeded and thinly sliced in strips	1	tablespoon balsamic vinegar
		½	cup extra-virgin olive oil
½	habañero pepper, seeded and minced	½	teaspoon salt
		½	teaspoon freshly ground black pepper
1	small clove garlic, crushed	½	teaspoon thyme
¼	cup minced pimento-stuffed olives	½	teaspoon oregano
3	tablespoons capers	¼	teaspoon marjoram
¾	cup shredded carrots	2	hard-boiled eggs, diced
½	cup cooked beets, diced		

1. Soak herring in a bowl of cool water overnight. Rinse and pick up any bones. Run through a food processor or mince by hand.

2. Combine herring, onion, peppers, garlic, olives, capers, carrots, beets, celery and parsley in a large non-reactive bowl, preferably glass or ceramic.

3. In a small bowl, stir together, vinegars, olive oil, salt, pepper and herbs. Pour over herring mixture and toss gently. Refrigerate overnight to marinate.

4. Toss gently again to mix ingredients, top with hard-boiled eggs.

Pea & Ham Soup (London Particular)

SERVES 4 TO 6

This hearty soup made its way over from England. It derives its name from the pea-soupers, those thick banks of fog that used to descend upon London. The addition of hot peppers gives it a West Indian flair.

1	tablespoon butter	1	small habañero pepper, seeded and minced
4	strips of lean bacon		
1	small onion, minced	1	pound split dried peas, rinsed
2	cloves garlic, crushed	2	quarts chicken broth
1	large carrot, thinly sliced	½	teaspoon freshly cracked black pepper
1	stalk celery, diced		

1. Fry the bacon in the butter along with the onion, garlic, carrot, celery and habañero pepper over moderate heat until onions are soft in a large soup pot. Remove one of the bacon slices to use as a garnish later. Drain on a white paper towel and set aside.

2. Add split peas and chicken broth. Bring to a boil, reduce heat, cover and simmer for 1 hour. Peas should be soft. Allow to cool for thirty minutes.

3. Puree in small batches in blender or food processor, taking care with hot liquid. Return to soup pot and gently reheat. Stir in black pepper. Ladle into individual bowls and garnish with crumbled bacon.

Conch Chowder (Tomato-Based)

SERVES 6 TO 8

When I moved to St. Thomas in my early twenties, there was a restaurant called "Gracie's" on Back Street, downtown Charlotte Amalie. The following is an adaptation of their recipe for what I consider the world's best conch chowder. It's changed a bit over the years as I experimented. Not bland, but not too fiery either. You can substitute any firm white fish or shell fish. I prefer crab, lobster or shrimp as it most resembles conch chewy texture. If you prefer not to use bacon, increase the garlic to 2 cloves, and the salt to 1 teaspoon.

2	pounds cooked, cleaned conch, run through a food mill or food processor	2	large carrots, thinly sliced
3	bacon strips, or 2 tablespoons olive oil	2	medium potatoes, peeled and cut in 1-inch pieces
1	large yellow onion, minced	1	bay leaf
1	garlic clove, crushed	2	tablespoons freshly shredded parsley
1	celery stalk, diced	1	teaspoon freshly shredded thyme, or
1	14-ounce can stewed, peeled tomatoes, with juice	½	teaspoon dried
		½	teaspoon dried oregano
¼	cup tomato paste	½	teaspoon salt
2	quarts chicken stock	½	teaspoon freshly cracked black pepper

1. Fry bacon until brown over medium-high heat. Remove and drain on paper towels. Drain all fat except 2 tablespoons. Sauté onion and garlic over moderate heat until lightly browned in bacon fat or olive oil if not using bacon. Add celery and cook another 3 to 5 minutes until soft.

2. Stir in canned tomatoes and tomato paste. Add chicken stock, carrots, bay leaf and potatoes. Bring to boil. Add conch meat and stir. Reduce heat, cover and simmer until vegetables are soft, about 25 minutes.

3. Add parsley, thyme and oregano. Simmer for 10 minutes. I prefer to add herbs toward the end of a recipe as they tend to lose flavor after lengthy cooking. Season to taste with salt and pepper.

Rich and Creamy Conch Chowder

MAKES 3 QUARTS

1	pound conch meat, cleaned	1	bay leaf
4	cups water	1	cup whole milk
2	ounces bacon or salt pork, minced	¾	cup half-and-half
2	medium yellow onions, minced	¼	cup evaporated milk
1	8-ounce bottle clam juice	2	tablespoons butter
2	large celery stalks, diced		salt
2	large potatoes, peeled and diced		black pepper

1. Run conch through a food mill or processor. Fill a deep kettle or stock pot with the 4 cups water. Add conch, cover and simmer for 1 and a half hours. Remove from heat and set aside.

2. Fry bacon in a large skillet until crisp. Remove bacon bits and set aside. Fry onion until lightly browned about 5 minutes.

3. Add clam juice to kettle. Stir in bacon, onion, celery, potatoes and bay leaf. Simmer, covered, for 20 minutes until potatoes are soft. Remove from heat.

4. Heat milk, half-and-half and evaporated milk in a separate saucepan until hot, but not boiling.

5. Stir milk mixture into kettle (do not bring to boil). Drop in butter and season to taste with salt and pepper.

Marina Cay

Owned by Pusser's West Indies, this charming little island is a short ferry ride, not far from Beef Island on Tortola, which also happens to be close to the airport. Situated on six acres, Marina Cay has a wonderful Pusser's Restaurant and comfortable hotel.

Mulligatawny Soup

SERVES 6

This fragrant, curried soup began in India when Britain ruled. Since then, there have been many variations. When slavery was abolished, East Indians migrated to Tortola and other Caribbean islands as indentured servants.

1 clove crushed garlic	2 large carrots, diced
1 teaspoon freshly grated ginger root	2½ quarts chicken stock
¼ teaspoon ground cumin	2/3 cup long-grain rice
¼ teaspoon ground cloves	2 sour apples, peeled, cored, diced
1 tablespoon curry powder	juice of one lime
¼ teaspoon cayenne pepper	2 tablespoons dry sherry
¼ cup butter	1 cup plain yogurt
1 4 pound roasting chicken, cut in serving pieces	2 tablespoons chopped coriander leaves
2 stalks celery, minced	½ cup heavy cream
1 large onion, minced	

1. Sauté garlic, ginger, cumin, cloves, curry powder and cayenne in the butter in a large skillet over moderate heat for 1 minute. Add chicken and brown on all sides.

2. Remove chicken with a slotted spoon and transfer to stock pot. Sauté celery, onion and carrots in skillet with butter and spices for 5 to 8 minutes until vegetables are soft. Scoop into stockpot with chicken.

3. Add chicken stock, bring to boil, reduce heat, cover and simmer for ½ hour. Remove chicken with slotted spoon and set aside. Add rice to pot, stir, and return to boil. Reduce heat, and cover until rice is cooked, following package directions.

4. When chicken has cooled, slice meat from bone into bite-size pieces. Discard skin and bones, and return to stock pot. Add apples and simmer over moderate heat for 12 minutes. Stir in yogurt.

5. Remove from heat, stir in lime juice, sherry, and heavy cream. Ladle into individual bowls. Garnish with coriander leaves.

Sage Mountain National Park

Sage Mountain is the British Virgin Island's tropical rainforest. This dense 92-acre forest offers trails through dense vegetation, with liana vines draping from evergreen trees, giant bromeliads clinging to fallen logs, and larger than life orchids. Drive through Road Town towards Cane Garden Bay, and just past the turn to Skyworld, take a right to the park and restaurant.

Pumpkin Soup with Chicken and Dumplings

SERVES 6

My housekeeper Viola introduced this recipe to me. Since then I've changed it, reduced the fat and sodium, but not the flavor. Children as well as adults enjoy this recipe, high in vitamin A and protein. Substitute winter squash, acorn squash or any other dark orange, firm pumpkin for the West Indian pumpkin. If you don't want to peel the pumpkin and chop it, prick all over with a fork, bake at 400° F for one hour until soft, then mash and use in recipe.

1 tablespoon olive oil	2 sprigs parsley
1 medium onion, minced	2 cups cooked, diced chicken meat, light and dark
4 cloves garlic, crushed	
2 quarts chicken stock	½ teaspoon freshly cracked black pepper
6 cups West Indian pumpkin, peeled, seeded and diced	sour cream
1 celery stalk, diced	ground nutmeg

1. Heat olive oil in a large stockpot. Sauté onion and garlic for 5 minutes until soft. Add pumpkin and cover with chicken broth. Add celery, bring to boil, reduce heat, and simmer until pumpkin is soft, about 20 minutes. Add parsley and simmer for 5 minutes. Remove from heat and allow to cool for 20 minutes.

2. Puree in blender or food processor until smooth. Add additional water as needed to thin out.

3. Return to stockpot. Add chicken, gently heating over moderate heat until chicken is heated through. Stir in pepper (do not add pepper any sooner, as cooking turns it bitter).

4. Add dumplings. Ladle into individual serving dishes. Top with dollop of sour cream, and sprinkle sparingly with nutmeg.

Dumplings

MAKES ABOUT 18

¾ cup all-purpose flour	¼ teaspoon ground cinnamon
½ cup finely ground cornmeal	3 tablespoons vegetable or olive oil
1 tablespoon sugar	¼ cup evaporated milk
½ teaspoon salt	

1. Sift flour into a medium bowl. Stir in cornmeal, sugar, salt and cinnamon. Add olive oil and evaporated milk. Knead into a soft dough, adding more flour or water as needed. Cover with a damp towel or piece of plastic wrap.

2. Heat a small pot of water to boiling. Drop in dumplings by teaspoonfuls and boil 20 to 25 minutes. Remove with slotted spoon and add to Pumpkin Soup and other soups and stews.

Kallaloo

SERVES 6

West Indians will catch land crabs, place them in a pen and feed them cornmeal and water for several days to purge the creatures. Since this is not always possible, and in the interest of time, I suggest you buy frozen or canned crabs. Kallaloo is served on 'Old Year's Night', a.k.a. New Year's Eve. Note: you don't need to use bacon or pork in this recipe. Substitute 2 tablespoons olive oil and an extra garlic clove instead.

6   ounces salt back pork, finely diced, or 4 strips of bacon
2   medium onions, minced
4   garlic cloves, crushed
½   jalapeño or habañero pepper, seeded and minced
1   stalk celery, diced
2   quarts chicken broth or stock
2   sprigs parsley, shredded
1   pound fresh or frozen okra, sliced in ¼-inch pieces
2   pounds crab meat (traditional), lobster or shrimp (all cooked)

1½ pounds fried fish fillets (see index), cut in 1-inch pieces
2   16-ounce package of fresh spinach or kallaloo leaves
1   teaspoon salt (add additional ½ teaspoon if not using pork or bacon)
1   teaspoon freshly cracked black pepper
¼   teaspoon ground cloves
¼   teaspoon ground nutmeg
¼   cup dry sherry

1. Fry the salt back pork or bacon in a deep stock pot until golden. Drain excess oil, remove bacon, crumble and set aside.

2. Sauté onion and garlic in bacon fat until soft. Add pepper and celery, continuing to cook over moderate heat for 2 minutes.

3. Add chicken stock, parsley and okra. Bring to boil, reduce heat, cover and simmer for 35 minutes. Fold in crab meat and spinach. Cover and simmer for 10 minutes. Add fried fish, salt, pepper, cloves, nutmeg and sherry. Cover and simmer for 10 minutes.

4. Remove from heat and allow to sit for 15 minutes. Serve with fungi (recipe follows).

Fungi

SERVES 6

Fungi reminds me of polenta. You can make it with or without okra. The secret to fungi is in the rapid, consistent stirring of the water and cornmeal.

1   cup stone-ground yellow cornmeal
1¾ cups water
1   tablespoon olive oil

1   tablespoon butter
1   teaspoon sugar
½   teaspoon salt

1. Bring water to boil in a medium sauce pan. Reduce heat, and gradually stir in cornmeal, beating rapidly.

2. Whisk in olive oil, butter, salt and sugar, stirring and cooking over moderate heat for 5 minutes.

3. Remove from heat. Serve alongside Kallaloo, soups, stews and fried fish.

Red Peas Soup with Dumplings

SERVES 8

Note, prepare dumpling dough (see index for recipe) ahead of time, so you can add to the soup shortly before serving.

1 pound dried red beans
8 ounces salt pork, or 3 slices bacon
2 quarts chicken stock
1 large yellow onion, minced
6 cloves garlic, minced
1 large stalk celery, diced
2 large carrots, thinly sliced
1 large sweet potato, diced in 1-inch cubes

1 large potato, red or white, diced in 1-inch cubes
1 bay leaf
1 to 2 quarts water as needed
¼ freshly shredded minced parsley
½ teaspoon black peppercorns

1. Place peas in deep kettle and cover with water. Bring to boil and cook for 10 minutes. Remove from heat, allow to cool. Drain, rinse and soak overnight. Drain in the morning, rinse again and place peas in stock pot. Add chicken stock and bring to boil. Reduce heat, cover and simmer for 1 hour.

2. Fry salt pork or bacon until brown on all sides in a medium skillet. Drain excess fat, reserving one tablespoon. Crumble bacon, or mince salt pork and set aside.

3. Sauté onion and garlic in remaining bacon fat. Transfer to stock pot. Add celery, carrots, sweet potato, potato, bay leaf and additional water. Return to boil, reduce heat and simmer for 15 minutes.

4. Form small dumplings (make these ahead of time) about the size of a bird egg, and drop into simmering soup. Add parsley and peppercorns, simmering for about 20 minutes. Remove bay leaf. Season to taste with salt. Serve soup hot with crusty bread.

Conch Salad

SERVES 6

2 pounds cooked conch, thinly sliced (see index)	¼ cup capers
1 medium yellow onion, thinly sliced	½ cup olive oil
3 garlic cloves, crushed	3 tablespoons apple-cider vinegar
½ small jalapeño or habañero pepper, seeded and minced	juice of one lime or lemon
2 large, vine ripened tomatoes, diced	3 tablespoons water
1 large green bell pepper, seeded and thinly sliced	1 teaspoon oregano
	½ teaspoon thyme
	½ teaspoon marjoram

1. Combine conch, onion, garlic, jalapeño pepper, tomatoes, bell pepper and capers in large, non-reactive bowl. Toss gently. Set aside.

2. Combine olive oil, vinegar, lemon juice, water, oregano, thyme and marjoram in a small cup. Pour over salad, toss gently to coat ingredients. Best if marinated overnight in the refrigerator.

Scallop Salad with Caramelized Onions

SERVES 4

To caramelize a vegetable means to change the carbon content of the sugar by long heat times. Instead of just sautéing onions for a few minutes, I'll take the extra time to get that exquisite caramelized flavor.

1½ pounds scallops	¼ cup sweet pickle relish
2 tablespoons apple cider vinegar	¼ cup fresh minced parsley
2 tablespoons olive oil	1 cup mayonnaise
1 large yellow onion, minced	salt
1 clove garlic, peeled and crushed	pepper
1 stalk celery, diced	

1. Boil scallops in a medium saucepan for 7 minutes. Drain, cool, dice and toss with vinegar. Chill in the refrigerator. Sauté onions in the olive oil over medium-high heat, stirring constantly until browned, about 20 minutes. Lower heat and keep cooking, stirring constantly, until onions are a luscious dark brown color, another 5 to 6 minutes. Remove from heat and cool.

2. Combine onion, garlic, celery, sweet pickle relish, parsley and mayonnaise in a large bowl. Fold in chilled scallops and cooled onions. Season to taste with salt and pepper. Serve on a bed of lettuce, with crusty bread and chilled white wine.

Mango-Ginger Coleslaw

SERVES 6

Fresh ginger has a much more pungent flavor than dried, which to me is a lackluster substitute. High in potassium, ginger has antiseptic properties, assists with fevers, reduces over eager appetites, and helps with indigestion and motion sickness.

6 cups shredded green cabbage	1 teaspoon Dijon-style mustard
1 cup shredded carrot	1 tablespoon freshly grated ginger
2 cups firm, yet ripe, diced mango	2 tablespoons capers
¾ cup mayonnaise	salt
1 teaspoon brown sugar	pepper

1. Toss cabbage, carrot and mango in a large, non-reactive bowl.

2. Combine mayonnaise, brown sugar, mustard and ginger in a separate small bowl. Fold into cabbage mixture. Gently mix in capers.

3. Season to taste with salt and pepper.

Virgin Gorda

Named the 'Fat Virgin' because Spanish sailors thought the island looked like a pregnant woman from a distance. The highest point is Gorda Peak at 1,370 feet in the north, mid-central section of the island.

Black Bean, Rice and Pineapple Salad

SERVES 6

Cuban-style black beans and rice make for a refreshing salad on sultry summer days. Pineapple adds sweetness, the hot peppers a touch of fire.

2 cups cooked black beans, or equivalent in canned (rinsed and drained)	¼ cup minced cilantro
	½ teaspoon cumin
	½ teaspoon oregano
2 cups cooked rice	1 small jalapeño pepper, seeded and minced
1 cup diced pineapple	
¼ cup chopped scallions	½ cup olive oil
¼ cup chopped chives	¼ cup Key Lime or lime juice
2 garlic cloves, crushed	salt
¼ cup chopped, pimento-stuffed green olives	pepper

1. Combine beans, rice, pineapple, scallions, chives, garlic, olives, cilantro, cumin, oregano and jalapeño peppers in a large, non-reactive bowl.

2. Drizzle olive oil and lime juice over salad. Toss gently. Season to taste with salt and pepper.

Tortola Beaches

Beaches in the British Virgin Islands in general are more secluded and unspoiled than those on St. Thomas or even St. Croix. On Tortola's north shore, you'll find crystal clear, aquamarine waters lapping deserted white sand beaches. All can be reached by vehicle, some though, on bumpy windy roads. For surfing, try **Apple Bay.** Snorkeler's will enjoy **Brewer's Bay** with its old distillery and sugar mill ruins. **Cane Garden Bay** is the Magens Bay of Tortola, a palm-rimmed stretch of beach complete with restaurants and bars. Have your camera ready once you round the hill of Long Bay Road for a stunning glimpse of **Long Bay. Elisabeth Beach** off of Ridge Road is a private beach accessible on foot; further along you'll find **Josiah's Bay,** often deserted, but take care with the undertow. **Smuggler's Cove** off of Belmont Road is stunning in its serenity, and directly north of Road Town is **Trunk Bay** where you'll need to hike down from Ridge Road.

Crab, Lobster, Snapper and other Seafood

Crab and Rice

SERVES 6 TO 8

The herb culantro is shaped like a long, sword-like serrated leaf. It resembles cilantro in flavor, only about 100 times stronger. Cilantro in your refrigerator will infuse everything with its delightful aroma. Adds a wonderful, bright and fresh taste to soups, stews and rice dishes. Try to use fresh herbs instead of dried whenever possible. You will need a mortar and pestle to make the sofrito paste that flavors this recipe.

2 pounds cooked crab meat, picked over for bones and cartilage
8 whole peppercorns
3 garlic cloves, crushed
1 large onion, minced
1½ teaspoons sea salt (coarse is best)
3 culantro leaves, or ¼ cup freshly shredded cilantro
½ cup freshly shredded parsley
1 tablespoon freshly shredded thyme, or 1 teaspoon dried

¼ cup olive oil
1 tablespoon annatto-infused olive oil (see sidebar)
1 stalk celery, diced
1½ cups white or basmati rice (more fragrant)
1 14-ounce can stewed, peeled tomatoes, with juice
2 tablespoons tomato paste
1½ quarts (6 cups) of low-sodium chicken broth

1. Place peppercorns in the bottom of a medium to large mortar and pestle. Add garlic, and use an up and down motion to pulverize the peppercorns.

2. Add ½ cup of the minced onion and continue to pound ingredients into a paste. Add salt, culantro leaves, parsley and thyme. Continuing pounding. Work in ¼ cup olive oil. Set aside.

3. Heat annatto-infused olive oil in the bottom of a deep kettle or Dutch oven. Sauté sofrito (peppercorn/garlic mixture) over moderate heat until vegetables are soft, about 3 to 5 minutes. Add celery and remaining onion. Continue to cook an additional 2 minutes.

4. Stir in rice, and stir until all grains are glistening with oil. This will seal the rice, and it will cook up fluffy. Pour in stewed tomatoes and tomato paste. Bring to boil, and then add chicken broth and crab. Bring to boil again, reduce heat, cover and simmer until all water is absorbed from rice.

5. Don't worry too much if you burn the rice on the bottom a bit. In Puerto Rico this is called pegao and is considered a specialty.

Annatto-Infused Olive Oil

It's easy to make your own annatto or achiote-infused olive oil. Use in place of regular olive oil to add an orange hue to food, and complex, smokey flavor. Heat 1 part annatto seeds to 2 parts vegetable oil over moderate heat until oil has turned bright red. Do not overheat oil. Strain and discard seeds.

Curried Lobster

SERVES 4 TO 6

Substitute any combination of shrimp or crab. For vegetarians, tofu replaces the shellfish nicely as it will absorb the spices and herbs.

2 strands saffron	1 tablespoon freshly grated ginger
2 teaspoons turmeric	2 cloves garlic, crushed
½ teaspoon freshly ground black pepper	2 tablespoons shredded cilantro
½ teaspoon coriander	1 small red bell pepper, seeded and cut in ¼-inch strips
½ teaspoon cumin	1 small green bell pepper, seeded and cut in ¼-inch strips
¼ teaspoon cinnamon	3 to 4 lobster tails (1 ½ pounds of shrimp or crab meat, or 1 block of extra-firm tofu, cut in ½-inch cubes)
¼ teaspoon cardamom	
¼ teaspoon ground mustard	
3 tablespoon olive oil	salt
1 medium onion, minced	

1. Crumble saffron into a ¼ cup of hot water. Set aside. Heat turmeric, black pepper, coriander, cumin, cinnamon, cardamom and mustard in the olive oil in a large skillet over medium heat for 1 minute. Add onion, garlic, cilantro, ginger, and bell peppers. Sauté for additional 3 minutes.

2. Chop lobster into bite-size pieces and add to skillet, stirring frequently. If using shrimp, crab (bite-size pieces) or tofu, toss in skillet, stirring well to coat with herbs and spices. Add saffron water. Sauté until lobster, crab or tofu are cooked about 7 to 10 minutes. Shrimp will have turned pink and curled slightly.

3. Serve over hot rice. Season to taste with salt.

Jost Van Dyke

This tiny jewel in the rough lies 4 miles northwest from West End, Tortola. Swim to Soggy Dollar bar, and visit with the 130 locals. Secluded and idyllic, with miles of powdery beaches.

Conch in Butter Sauce

SERVES 6

My ex-husband introduced me to this dish when I moved to St. Thomas. Hardly low-cal, but certainly islandy and delicious. I've cut the amount of butter in half and substituted an equal amount of olive oil for a more health-conscious choice.

2 pounds of cooked, cleaned conch (see index), thinly sliced	1 small green bell pepper, seeded and thinly sliced
juice of 1 lime	1 stalk celery, diced
½ cup apple-cider vinegar	½ small habañero pepper, seeded and minced
1 tablespoon olive oil	
1 large yellow onion, minced	4 tablespoons butter
3 garlic cloves, crushed	4 tablespoons olive oil
1 small red bell pepper, seeded and thinly sliced	½ cup water
	½ cup chicken broth

1. Soak conch slices in lime juice and vinegar for 1 hour. Place in pressure cooker, cover with a small amount of water and cook for 30 minutes. Drain water and set aside.

2. Sauté onion and garlic in 1 tablespoon olive oil over moderate heat for 2 minutes. Add pepper strips, celery and habañero pepper. Cook for additional 3 minutes.

3. Add butter, olive oil, water and chicken broth along with pressure-cooked conch. Reduce heat and simmer for 12 minutes. Stir in fresh lime juice. Serve over hot rice, with boiled green bananas, fried plantains and potato stuffing.

Fried Snapper

SERVES 4

4 6-ounce fillets of snapper, grouper or mahi-mahi	vegetable or olive oil for frying
¾ cup milk	salt
1 cup seasoned breadcrumbs	pepper

1. Heat 1-inch of olive oil in a deep skillet to 375° F. Rinse fish fillets under cool, running water and pat dry.

2. Dip fish in milk, and then roll in breadcrumbs. Shake off excess. Fry until golden on both sides. Do not overcrowd pan as this will lower heat of oil and cause fish to soak up too much fat. Drain on food-grade white paper towels. Season to taste with salt and pepper.

Creole Fish

SERVES 4

Haul out the mortar and pestle to make the seasoning for this recipe.

4   6-ounce fillets fried grouper, mahi-mahi
    or snapper (see preceding recipe)
8   whole peppercorns
3   garlic cloves, crushed
1   small onion, minced
1½ teaspoons sea salt (coarse is best)
3   culantro leaves, or ¼ cup freshly
    shredded cilantro
½   cup freshly shredded parsley
1   tablespoon freshly shredded thyme,
    or 1 teaspoon dried

3   tablespoons cup olive oil
1   large yellow onion, thinly sliced
2   stalks celery, diced
1   red bell pepper, seeded and sliced in
    thin strips
1   14-ounce can stewed tomatoes with
    juice
3   tablespoons tomato paste
2   tablespoons minced pimento-stuffed
    olives
2   tablespoons capers

1. Place peppercorns in bottom of mortar. Add garlic and pulverize peppercorns using an up and down motion. Add salt, minced onion, cilantro, parsley and thyme, continuing with pounding motion. Work in olive oil.

2. Scrape mixture into a deep, heavy skillet. Sauté over moderate heat for 3 minutes. Add onion slices, celery and red pepper. Cook for additional 3 minutes.

3. Pour in stewed tomatoes and paste. Add reserved fish, olives and capers; cover and simmer over low heat for 15 minutes. Serve over rice, with fungi, fried plantain or boiled bananas.

Curried Salt Fish and Rice

SERVES 6

1½ pounds boneless salt fish
2   teaspoons turmeric
½   teaspoon freshly ground black
    pepper
½   teaspoon coriander
½   teaspoon cumin
¼   teaspoon cinnamon
¼   teaspoon cardamom
¼   teaspoon ground mustard
3   tablespoon olive oil

1   medium onion, thinly sliced
1   tablespoon freshly grated ginger
2   cloves garlic, crushed
2   tablespoons shredded cilantro
1   small red bell pepper, seeded and
    cut in ¼-inch strips
1   small green bell pepper, seeded and
    cut in ¼-inch strips
1½ cups rice
1   8-ounce can stewed tomatoes

1. Soak salt fish over night in a bowl of water in the refrigerator. Drain, rinse and soak for additional 2 hours to remove excess salt. Drain and flake apart with fingers. Set aside.

2. Sauté turmeric, black pepper, coriander, cumin, cinnamon, cardamom and mustard in olive oil over moderate heat for 1 minute. Add onion, ginger and garlic. Continue to cook for 3 minutes, stirring constantly. Fold in cilantro and bell pepper strips, stirring over medium heat for 2 minutes.

3. Add rice, stirring to coat rice with oil. Add stewed tomatoes, water and salt fish. Stir, fold in reserved fish, then reduce heat, cover and simmer until all water is absorbed from rice (time depending upon which rice used).

Dolphin Baked in Mango Honey

SERVES 4

½ cup honey	1 cup cubed fresh mango
juice of 1 Key lime or a lemon	¼ teaspoon ground cinnamon
½ cup white wine	2 pounds dolphin fillets
¼ cup orange liqueur, such as	salt
Cointreau, Triple Sec or Grand	pepper
Marnier	

1. Preheat oven to 350°. Combine honey, lime juice, wine, orange liqueur, mango and cinnamon in a medium bowl.

2. Lightly oil the bottom of a 9x12-inch glass baking dish. Arrange dolphin fillets over bottom. Top with mango mixture. Bake for 30 minutes until fish flakes easily.

3. Season to taste with salt and pepper.

Lime-Coconut Fried Lobster

SERVES 4

Sound too rich to be true? Lightly frying lobster seals in its wonderful sweet flavor and keeps it from drying out. Be sure to heat the oil to 350°, otherwise the batter will soak up too much oil. Also, do not overcrowd pan, as this will lower oil temperature as well.

4 Florida or Caribbean lobster tails	1 cup all-purpose flour
juice of 2 Key limes or lemons	1 teaspoon salt
½ cup condensed milk (unsweetened)	½ teaspoon cracked black pepper
½ cup unsweetened coconut milk	¾ cup shredded, unsweetened coconut
2 eggs, beaten	vegetable oil for frying

1. Remove meat from shell and slice down center back (but not all the way through) with the tip of a sharp knife. Drizzle with lemon juice and place in a non-reactive glass baking dish to marinate for thirty minutes.

2. Combine condensed milk, coconut milk and eggs in a small bowl. Combine flour, salt and black pepper in another bowl. Place shredded coconut in a third bowl.

3. Heat ½-inch of oil in a large skillet to 350°.

4. Dip lobster tails in flour, then egg, then shredded coconut. Shake off excess.

5. Fry tails 2 at time until golden on both sides, about 5 to 8 minutes. Drain on food-grade white paper towels.

6. Serve at once with drawn butter, mustard sauce or chutney.

Grilled Yellowtail Snapper with Black Bean, Mango and Coconut Salsa

SERVES 6

2 pounds yellowtail snapper fillets (check other recipes)	1 tablespoon balsamic vinegar
½ cup minced onion	1 tablespoon rum
2 large cloves garlic, minced	½ teaspoon salt
½ cup olive oil	½ teaspoon freshly cracked black pepper
juice of 2 Key limes	

SALSA:

1 cup cooked black beans (firm, not mushy)	¼ cup olive oil
1 cup diced fresh mango	¼ cup cider vinegar
½ cup minced onion	1 tablespoon honey
1 small ripe tomato, diced	½ teaspoon cinnamon
½ cup unsweetened, shredded coconut	½ teaspoon salt
¼ cup minced cilantro	½ teaspoon freshly cracked black pepper

1. Combine onion, garlic, olive oil, lime juice, vinegar, rum, salt and black pepper in a small bowl. Arrange fish fillets on the bottom of a 9x12-inch glass baking dish. Pour marinade over top and allow to sit for 1 hour.

2. Combine black beans, mango, onion, tomato, coconut, cilantro, olive oil, vinegar, honey, cinnamon, salt and black pepper in a large, non-reactive bowl. Cover with plastic wrap and refrigerate.

3. Preheat grill for 10 minutes to medium-high heat. Grill snapper for 5 minutes on each side.

4. Serve with Black Bean, Mango and Coconut Salsa.

Caribbean Baked Snapper

SERVES 4

3	pounds snapper fillets	1	bay leaf
½	cup olive oil	2	large yellow onions, thinly sliced
¼	cup sherry	2	large ripe tomatoes, thinly sliced
¼	cup white wine	2	green bell peppers, seeded and diced
	juice of 3 limes or lemons		
1	tablespoon apple cider vinegar	¼	cup pimento-stuffed green olives, chopped
2	tablespoons tomato paste		
3	garlic cloves crushed	2	tablespoons capers
1	teaspoon Italian seasoning		

1. Combine olive oil, sherry, white wine, lemon juice, vinegar and tomato paste in a small, non-reactive bowl. Fold in garlic and Italian seasoning. Set aside.

2. Place snapper fillets in a 9x12-inch glass baking dish. Place bay leaf in dish. Arrange onions, tomatoes, bell pepper, olives and capers over fish. Drizzle with olive oil sauce.

3. Preheat oven to 375°. Bake 20 to 20-5 minutes until fish flakes easily.

Spicy Shrimp Pasta with Coconut Avocado Butter

SERVES 4 TO 6

3	pounds large shrimp, shelled and deveined	1	tablespoon soy sauce
		1	tablespoon cayenne pepper
	juice of 1 Key lime or lemon	½	teaspoon cumin
3	tablespoons apple cider vinegar	1	teaspoon salt
3	tablespoons frozen orange juice concentrate, thawed	1	teaspoon freshly cracked black pepper
1	tablespoon toasted sesame oil	1	tablespoon olive oil

COCONUT AVOCADO BUTTER		2	tablespoons fresh minced cilantro
2	large ripe avocados, peeled and pitted	½	cup unsweetened coconut milk
			juice of 1 lime or lemon
	juice of 1 lime or lemon	1	pound angel hair pasta or pasta of choice
1	small yellow onion, minced		
2	cloves garlic, crushed	1	tablespoon olive oil

1. Combine lime juice, vinegar, orange juice concentrate, sesame oil, soy sauce, cayenne, cumin, salt and black pepper in a 9x12-inch glass baking dish. Toss and coat shrimp with marinade. Set aside for thirty minutes.

2. Sprinkle lime juice over avocado to keep it from turning brown. In a large bowl, combine onion, garlic, cilantro and coconut milk.

3. Fold in avocado and beat with a hand held mixer until smooth. Drizzle with remaining juice of lime or lemon.

4. Heat 1 tablespoon of olive oil in a large heavy skillet over moderate heat. Transfer shrimp and marinade to skillet. Cook, stirring occasionally until shrimp are pink on all sides. About 5 minutes. Check for doneness on inside by slicing into 1 shrimp. Remove from heat, cover and place in a warm spot.

5. Cook pasta according to package directions. Drain and toss with 1 tablespoon of olive oil.

6. Toss pasta with Coconut Avocado butter. Top with shrimp.

The Baths

Virgin Gorda's most unusual feature is an area south of Spanish Town (the original capital of the British Virgin Islands) strewn with giant, house-size boulders, some submerged in sand, others completely in the water. Millions of years ago, crystalline granite boulders formed when molten rock was forced up, and became trapped between layers of rock. A layer of cooled granite produced, and after millenniums of the earth shifting, cracks appeared. Eventually erosion by sea and sand formed rounded corners and giant rocks.

Sunlit caves, with sand floors, can be explored safely. The National Trust has facilitated exploration with rope and wooden ladders. An eerie, yet hauntingly beautiful area, with tropical flowers and swaying palms. Wonderful beach for swimming and a number of unusual gift shops and bars which serve tasty food and drinks.

Chicken and Meat

Chicken and Chickpea Rotis

MAKES 10

"Roti" or "Chapati" is an Indian flatbread that made its way up from Trinidad. The roti is rolled out like dough, then cooked on a griddle. It's quite quick and simple to make as it requires little kneading and doesn't require time to rise. Make dough ahead of time and refrigerate to save time. You can purchase ground chickpeas at the health food store.

2 tablespoons vegetable oil	½ cup shredded white cabbage
1½ teaspoons turmeric	1 cup water
½ teaspoon ground black pepper	2 tablespoons dry sherry
½ teaspoon salt	
½ teaspoon cumin	½ cup all-purpose flour
½ teaspoon allspice	½ cup ground chickpea flour or
½ teaspoon ground ginger	cornmeal
¼ teaspoon ground mustard	1 teaspoon sea salt
1 small onion, minced	1 tablespoon oil or ghee (clarified
1 garlic clove, crushed	butter)
1 cup cooked, diced chicken meat	1 to 4 tablespoons milk (depending on
1 cup cooked chickpeas (canned is	humidity)
fine	extra flour for dusting rolling surface
1 medium potato, peeled and diced	

1. For filling: Heat oil in a large skillet over moderate heat. Sauté spices for five minutes, stirring often. Toss in onion and garlic, and cook for additional five minutes. Fold in chicken, chickpeas, potatoes and cabbage. Cook for 1 minute.

2. Add water and sherry. Cover, reduce heat and simmer for 15 minutes until vegetables are soft, but not mushy. Remove from heat, cover and keep warm.

3. For roti wrapper: Sift together flours and sea salt into a large bowl. Drizzle oil over flour and work into flour with your fingers.

4. Add milk, a small amount at a time, working mixture with your hands. Once you've got it into a ball, stop kneading. You'll have a stiff dough, similar to pizza dough.

5. Divide the dough in thirds. Roll out a small portion on a flour dusted surface until dough is the thickness of a slice of American cheese. Cut out a six-inch round. Repeat with remaining dough.

6. Preheat a heavy frying over moderate heat. Place roti round on hot surface, and cook for one minute. Flip. Roti is done when you have some light brown spots. Oil skillet in between rotis. Keep rotis warm until all are cooked.

7. Scoop chicken curry onto roti, fold and serve at once. It's OK to use your hands to eat.

Chicken and Rice

SERVES 8

1 ounce salt pork, minced
1 tablespoon olive oil (note if not using saffron, use annatto-infused olive oil (see sidebar)
1 whole 3-4 pound chicken, cut up with skin on (or assorted breasts and legs)
1 large onion, minced
6 cloves garlic, crushed
1 small red bell pepper, minced
1 small green bell pepper, minced
3 cups long-grain rice
1 16-ounce can tomatoes, drained and chopped

¼ teaspoon red pepper flakes
4 cups chicken broth
2 cups beer
½ cup dry sherry
12 saffron threads
2 small bay leaves
1 teaspoon freshly cracked black pepper
½ teaspoon oregano
½ teaspoon thyme
1 small can peas, drained
1 jar roasted red peppers

1. Heat the salt pork and olive oil in a large deep skillet over moderate heat. Add chicken and brown on all sides. Remove chicken and reserve.

2. Stir in onion, garlic, and bell peppers, sautéing until onion is soft. Fold in rice, cooking for 2 minutes until rice is glistening from the oil. Add tomatoes, pepper flakes, chicken broth, beer and sherry. Bring to a boil, crumble in saffron, add bay leaves, black pepper, oregano and thyme, stirring for thirty seconds.

3. Arrange chicken on top of dish, reduce heat and cover tightly. Simmer until all water is absorbed from rice, about 20 minutes.

4. Turn rice from top to bottom using large forks or spoons. Top with peas and roasted red peppers. Cover and allow to sit for 10 minutes. Serve with fried plantain and a green salad.

Curried Chicken

SERVES 6

1 3-pound serving chicken, cut in pieces
1 tablespoon curry powder
½ teaspoon cumin
½ teaspoon cinnamon
½ teaspoon ground red pepper
1 tablespoon chicken seasoning
2 tablespoons olive oil
1 large onion, minced

2 large ripe tomatoes, chopped
¾ cup chicken stock
¼ cup sherry
¼ cup unsweetened coconut milk
3 tablespoons flour
2 tablespoons butter
½ teaspoon hot pepper sauce
salt
pepper

1. Rinse chicken under cool, running water, pat dry and set aside.

2. Heat curry powder, cumin, cinnamon, red pepper and chicken seasoning in a large skillet or Dutch oven for 2 minutes until slightly darkened and a fragrant aroma is released.

3. Add olive oil and sauté onion until just soft. Add chicken pieces, tomatoes, stock, sherry and coconut milk. Cover and simmer over moderate heat for 20 minutes.

4. Heat butter in a separate small pot or skillet over moderate heat until melted. Sprinkle in flour, stirring constantly, until a golden color and a nutty aroma is emitted. Stir in hot pepper sauce.

5. Fold this roux into chicken mixture, stirring until thickened. Simmer for 7 to 8 minutes. Serve with fluffy white rice and green vegetables.

Necker Island

Necker Island is to the north of Virgin Gorda, across Virgin Sound. This private island is owned by Richard Branson, owner of Virgin Atlantic airline. Accommodations are fabulous, a Great House with 10 enormous bedrooms, and two Balinese cottages. You and 23 friends can stay if you rent the entire island, which includes five beaches, secluded paths, tennis courts and private chef.

Jerked Chicken

SERVES 6

This method of cooking made its way to the Virgin Islands, the rest of the Caribbean and Florida via Jamaica by way of the Carib-Arawak Indians. The Indians would line a deep pit with wood and stones, which would add a smokey flavor. A small animal or bird was 'jerked' by poking with small holes that would then be stuffed with spices, and roasted slowly over low heat. The end result was a wonderfully spicy, moist meat.

1	cup olive oil	¼	cup apple cider vinegar
1	large onion, minced		juice of 1 Key lime or regular lime
2	habañero or Scotch bonnet peppers, seeded and minced	¼	cup brown sugar
		1	tablespoon ground allspice
2	tablespoons fresh ginger	1	teaspoon dried sage
2	teaspoons dried thyme	½	teaspoon ground cinnamon
4	large garlic cloves, crushed	½	teaspoon ground nutmeg
½	cup orange juice	3	pounds chicken breasts or thighs

1. Combine all ingredients except chicken thighs in a food processor. Baste and marinate chicken overnight in a glass baking dish.

2. Preheat barbeque grill to low to medium heat. Or, set oven to 300°. Barbeque or bake chicken slowly until juices run clear when cut.

Spanish-Style Roast Garlic Chicken

SERVES 6

1	4 to 5 pound chicken	2	tablespoons olive oil
10	cloves garlic, peeled	2	teaspoons oregano
2	large lemons	½	teaspoon cumin
	paprika	½	cup fresh lime juice
1	teaspoon salt	¼	cup frozen orange juice concentrate, thawed
1	teaspoon freshly cracked black pepper		oregano

1. Rinse chicken inside and out. Pat dry. Quarter 1 lemon and place inside body cavity along with 4 cloves or garlic. Cut other lemon in half and rub on outside of chicken.

2. Sprinkle chicken lightly with paprika, then salt, then pepper. Set aside.

3. Combine olive oil, oregano, cumin, lime juice, frozen orange juice concentrate and oregano in a small bowl. Crush remaining 6 cloves of garlic and add to bowl.

4. Baste chicken with marinade. Cover with plastic wrap and marinate overnight in the refrigerator.

5. Preheat oven to 375° F. Place chicken on a roasting pan, reserving marinade. Bake for 65 to 75 minutes, basting several times with marinade. Remove when done, i.e. juice run clear when the thickest portion of the thigh is pierced. Discard any unused marinade, i.e. uncooked, as it may contain bacteria.

Daube Meat

SERVES 6 TO 8

Daube means Creole. Any type of meat may be used, but I find lamb to be the most flavorful and tender.

2 pounds beef, lamb or pork cut up for stew	1 large yellow onion, thinly sliced
juice of 2 limes	4 garlic cloves, crushed
2 tablespoons vinegar	1 stalk celery, diced
1 teaspoon salt	1 14-ounce can stewed tomatoes with juice
½ teaspoon freshly cracked black pepper	3 tablespoons tomato paste
1 teaspoon paprika	3 tablespoons apple-cider vinegar
1 teaspoon thyme	2 tablespoons dry sherry
½ teaspoon cayenne pepper	1 bay leaf
3 tablespoons olive oil	3 whole cloves
	1 cup of water (as needed)

1. Sprinkle meat with lime juice and vinegar. Season with salt, black pepper, paprika, thyme and cayenne. Cover and refrigerate over night to tenderize.

2. Heat olive oil in a deep kettle. Drain any excess lime juice from meat. Brown on all sides over medium heat. Add onion slices, garlic and celery. Sauté for 3 minutes.

3. Stir in stewed tomatoes, tomato paste, vinegar, sherry, bay leaf and cloves. Add water as needed to make a gravy. Reduce heat to very low, cover and simmer for 45 to 60 minutes. The idea is a long, slow cooking time. Serve with hot rice, plantains and baked yams.

Puerto Rican-Style Roast Pork

SERVES 12

You'll find Spanish-speaking immigrants all over the islands, even the British Virgin Islands. Here are their lovely contributions to BVI cuisine.

5 to 6 pound pork roast	2 crumbled bay leaves
12 garlic cloves, thinly sliced	1 teaspoon oregano
1 cup fresh lemon juice	1 teaspoon rosemary
½ cup shredded fresh culantro if available; or cilantro, or 2 tablespoons dried	salt pepper

1. Make slits all over the roast with the tip of a sharp knife. Insert garlic.

2. Combine lemon juice, cilantro, bay leaves, oregano and rosemary in a small bowl. Pour over roast and marinate overnight in the refrigerator.

3. Heat oven to 325° F. Place roast in a Dutch oven. Roast for 3 hours or until a meat thermometer inserted in center of roast reads 165° F.

4. Allow roast to rest for 15 minutes before serving. Season to taste with salt and pepper.

Ropa Vieja

SERVES 6

This meat stew is tasty and quick to prepare. And it makes the house smell wonderful! Serve with hot white rice, black beans and fried plantains.

3 pounds flank steak, cut into 3 by 4 inch strips, or boneless beef round roast	1 small green pepper, minced
	1 cup tomato sauce
	¼ cup vinegar
3 tablespoons olive oil	1 cup water
4 garlic cloves, crushed	1 cup sofrito sauce (see index)
1 small onion, minced	

1. Heat oil in a large saucepan and brown meat on all sides. Remove meat from skillet and reserve.

2. Sauté garlic, onion and green pepper until soft, about 5 minutes. Stir in tomato sauce, water and sofrito.

3. Return to pot, cover and simmer on very, very low heat (about 2 hours) until meat shreds easily, like old clothes. Add additional water as needed.

Tropical Meat Pie

SERVES 6 TO 8

This recipe is an adaptation of a recipe by my ex-husband, Richard.

1 tablespoon olive oil	1 teaspoon salt
1 small onion, minced	1 teaspoon dried oregano
3 cloves garlic, crushed	½ teaspoon dried thyme
1 medium bell pepper, seeded and minced	½ teaspoon freshly cracked black pepper
1 pound extra lean hamburger meat	¾ cup shredded cheddar cheese
¾ cup tomato sauce	1 pre-made pie shell
2 tablespoons apple cider vinegar	
2 tablespoons minced jalapeño peppers	

1. Heat olive oil in large skillet over medium heat. Sauté onion, garlic and bell pepper until soft. Crumble in ground beef. Stir constantly until no pink remains. Transfer to a metal or wire colander and rinse off excess fat with hot water. Rinse out skillet with hot water.

2. Return hamburger/onion mixture to skillet. Stir in tomato sauce, vinegar, jalapeño peppers, salt, oregano, thyme and black pepper.

3. Preheat oven to 350°. Transfer hamburger mixture to pie shell. Top with shredded cheese.

4. Bake thirty-five to forty-five minutes until crust is golden and cheese is bubbly.

Anegada

Anegada, north of Virgin Gorda, is a flat coral and limestone island, unlike the other volcanic and hilly Virgin Islands. Nine miles long, and two miles wide, the island barely reaches 30 feet in sea level. It's been said, by the time you see the island, you'll have run your boat into a reef, and indeed more than 300 sea captains have already done so. The reefs are a snorkeler's and scuba diver's paradise, viewing one coral formation after another and scores of brilliant tropical fish. You'll find sugar-fine sand beaches, a comfortable hotel, and a handful of delightful eateries and water holes among the island's population of fewer than 200.

Shepherd's Pie, Tortola-Style

SERVES 6

There's a good bit of controversy over the recipe 'Shepherd's Pie.' Some folks claim Shepherd's Pie is made with lamb, while Cottage Pie is made from beef. Nonetheless, the Caribbean version of the pie utilizes lamb or beef interchangeably, but with the kick of hot peppers. Lamb chops needn't be a rare, expensive treat. Substitute budget-priced shoulder chops with their rich flavor, and slightly chewy texture.

¾ pound lamb shoulder chops, or beef chuck, cubed in 1-inch pieces
2 tablespoons olive oil
1 medium yellow onion, minced
½ habañero pepper, seeded and minced
½ pound mushrooms, washed and sliced
2 carrots, scraped and thinly sliced
3 tablespoons flour
½ cup, plus 2 tablespoons beef stock

4 tablespoons dark rum
2 tablespoons tomato paste
1 tablespoon cider vinegar
½ bay leaf
2 large potatoes, boiled and peeled
2 tablespoons butter, melted
1 tablespoon dried parsley, or 2 tablespoons fresh, shredded
½ cup evaporated milk
¾ cup grated, sharp-yellow cheddar

1. Preheat oven to 375°F. Mince lamb or beef in a food processor. Sauté lamb, onion, habañero pepper, mushrooms and carrots in olive oil in a large skillet over moderate heat for 10 minutes.

2. Sprinkle in flour, stirring constantly over medium heat for 3 minutes, until mixture is slightly thickened. Whisk in beef stock, rum, tomato paste and vinegar. Add bay leaf. Cover, reduce heat and simmer for 20 minutes.

3. Mash potatoes with melted butter, parsley and evaporated milk. Set aside.

4. Scoop meat mixture into the bottom of an oven-proof dish. Top with mashed potatoes. Top with grated cheddar. Bake for 20 minutes until bubbly.

Scallop and Mushroom Pie

SERVES 10

Scallops have a delicate flavor, which blends well with other fish. Perfect for fussy, non-seafood eaters. In Ireland this dish is baked and served in single-serving scallop-shaped dishes.

1	medium yellow onion, minced	1	cup whole milk, divided
1	small garlic clove, crushed	2	large potatoes, boiled and peeled
2	tablespoons olive oil	¼	teaspoons nutmeg
½	pound fresh scallops, large size	½	pound mushrooms
1	pound snapper fillets, cut in 1-1/2-inch pieces	7	tablespoons butter, divided
1	bay leaf	3	tablespoons flour
½	teaspoon paprika	¼	cup dry sherry
½	cup evaporated milk	¾	cup breadcrumbs
		¼	cup shredded fresh parsley

1. Preheat oven to 350°F. Sauté onion and garlic in the olive oil in a medium saucepan over moderate heat for 5 minutes until soft.

2. Slice scallops thinly. Place scallops and snapper in medium saucepan with onion, bay leaf, paprika, evaporated milk and ½ cup of the whole milk. Simmer over low heat until fish is tender, about 12 minutes. Remove from heat and reserve.

3. Mash potatoes along with remaining ½ cup of milk and nutmeg, and set aside. Scoop fish and scallops from milk. Reserve milk. Set both aside, discarding bay leaf.

4. Fry mushrooms in 4 tablespoons of the butter in a small saucepan over medium heat. Sprinkle in flour, stirring constantly, until lightly browned and a nutty aroma is given off. Whisk in reserved milk. Stir until slightly thickened, about 3 minutes. Stir in sherry, scallops and fish. Combine gently and remove from heat.

5. Spoon scallops into an oven-proof dish. Top with fish mixture.

6. Melt remaining 3 tablespoons butter in a small skillet. Toss in breadcrumbs and parsley, stirring well. Cook over medium heat for 1 minute. Sprinkle breadcrumbs over fish. Bake for 20 to 25 minutes until bubbly.

Meat Patés (Meat Pastry)

MAKES 10

For peak flavor, use fresh herbs instead of dried, for these to die-for meat pastries. Whenever our family took a trip off island, we would stop at the mobile food wagon across from the airport to pick up these spicy fritters. Note, you can bake these instead of frying if you like.

1½ **pounds minced beef**	1 **teaspoon freshly cracked black**
3 **tablespoons minced parsley**	**pepper**
2 **tablespoons minced chives**	2 **cups flour**
1 **tablespoons minced thyme**	1 **tablespoon baking powder**
2 **tablespoons olive oil**	½ **teaspoon salt**
1 **small onion, minced**	1 **teaspoon curry powder**
2 **garlic cloves, crushed**	½ **cup shortening**
1 **small habanero pepper, minced**	2 **tablespoons chilled butter, cut in**
1 **tablespoon tomato paste**	**small pieces**
1 **tablespoon vinegar**	½ **cup water, more or less depending**
1 **teaspoon salt**	**on humidity**

1. For filling: Fold herbs into meat. Heat oil in a large skillet or saucepan. Add meat, and cook over moderate heat, stirring constantly for 5 minutes. Add onions, garlic, pepper, tomato paste, vinegar, salt and pepper. Sauté for additional 15 minutes, until meat is cooked. Set aside.

2. For pastry: Sift together flour, baking powder, salt and curry powder. Cut in shortening and butter with a pastry cutter or fork until mixture resembles pebbles. Add water in small amounts using your hands until a ball is formed.

3. Roll out dough on a floured surfaced until the thickness of a thick slice of American cheese.

4. Cut in five inch squares. Place filling in center and fold over into a triangle, pressing down edges with tines of a fork.

5. Either brush tops with beaten egg, and bake in a 350°F oven for 30 minutes; or heat one-inch of vegetable oil to 350°F. Fry patés one at a time until golden. Drain on food-grade white paper towels. Serve with hot sauce.

Vegetables, Fritters and Sides

West Indian Johnny Cakes

SERVES 6

2½ cups sifted flour
1½ teaspoons baking powder
1 teaspoon sugar
½ teaspoon salt

1/3 cup vegetable shortening
¼ cup milk
¾ cup water
vegetable oil for frying

1. Sift together all dry ingredients. Cut shortening into dry ingredients just like you would for a pie crust (use pastry cutter or two knives) until mixture resembles crumbly sand.

2. Gradually work in water and milk until a soft dough forms. Knead gently until dough becomes smooth and elastic. Cover bowl and place in a warm place for 30 minutes.

3. Flatten with a rolling pin to ½-inch thickness on a heavily floured surface. Cut out with a biscuit cutter.

4. Heat oil to 360° F. Fry cakes until golden, taking care not to overcrowd pan. Drain on food-grade white paper towels. Serve with hot sauce or dust with granulated sugar.

Guana Island

Guana Island is a very private, and very secluded island owned by a small resort. Access is limited to the launch the hotel sends for its guests. Fifteen, Caribbean-inspired guest rooms in seven houses are complete with their own porch, and fabulous down-island views. Tropical fauna abounds on the island along its six deserted beaches.

Potato Stuffing

SERVES 8 TO 10

Virtually every West Indian gathering will offer this filling and tasty dish. An inexpensive investment in a potato ricer will make fluffy, not gluey stuffing.

6 large white potatoes, peeled and diced 1 teaspoon salt	1 tablespoon olive oil or bacon fat
¼ cup butter or olive oil	1 large yellow onion, minced
¼ cup evaporated milk	1 large sweet red bell pepper, minced
¼ cup whole milk	½ small habañero pepper, minced
2 tablespoons brown sugar	1 teaspoon dried thyme
2 tablespoons ketchup	½ teaspoon dried marjoram
1 tablespoon tomato paste	½ cup raisins

1. Place potatoes in a large, deep kettle or saucepan. Add salt and cover with water. Bring to a boil, reduce heat and simmer until potatoes are soft, about 20 minutes. Drain.

2. Run potatoes through a potato ricer or mash gently. Add butter, milks, brown sugar, ketchup and tomato paste. Set aside.

3. Heat olive oil in a large skillet. Sauté onion, bell pepper and habañero pepper until soft, about 3 to 5 minutes over medium heat. Stir in thyme, marjoram and raisins. Simmer for 2 minutes.

4. Preheat oven to 350° F. Combine onion with mashed potato mixture. Spoon into a greased baking dish. Bake for 20 to 25 minutes until golden.

Soda Scones

MAKES ABOUT 12

Scones are not traditionally made with spices. However, in the Caribbean islands, spices grow plentifully, and made their way into all sorts of recipes with delightful results.

2 cups flour	pinch of cardamom (optional)
1 teaspoon sugar	pinch of cinnamon (optional)
½ teaspoon salt	4 tablespoons chilled butter, cut in
½ teaspoon baking soda	small pieces
½ teaspoon cream of tartar	¾ cup of milk more or less

1. Preheat oven to 450°F. Lightly grease a baking sheet.

2. Sift all dry ingredients together into a large bowl. Cut in butter with either a pastry cutter, or a fork until mixture is crumbly like sand.

3. Work in just enough milk (depending on moisture content of flour) to make a stiff dough. Form into a ball and turn out onto a floured surface.

4. Roll into about ½-inch thickness. Cut into triangles. Bake for 8 to 10 minutes until just golden.

Banana Fritters

SERVES 4 TO 6

1½ cups all-purpose flour
½ teaspoon salt
3 teaspoons baking powder
½ teaspoon ground cinnamon
¼ teaspoon cardamom
2 large ripe bananas, mashed
1 egg, lightly beaten

¼ cup granulated sugar
1 tablespoon brown sugar
1 teaspoon vanilla extract
½ cup evaporated milk
¾ cup water
vegetable oil for frying

1. Sift together all dry ingredients. Set aside.

2. Combine banana, egg, sugars, vanilla, milks and water in a large bowl. Work in dry ingredients. You should have a smooth batter.

3. Heat oil to 360° F. Drop by large tablespoonfuls into hot fat. Fry until golden. Drain on white paper towels.

Fried Plantain

SERVES 4

Plantains belong to the banana family, and when cooked taste nearly identical. Serve alongside fish, meat or jerked dishes.

2 large ripe plantain (yellow with black flecks)

1 tablespoon butter
1 tablespoon olive oil

1. Slice the end off each plantain and peel like a banana. Cut in ½-inch diagonal slices.

2. Heat oil in large skillet over medium heat, until hot but not smoking. Sauté plantain on each side, about 3 minutes until golden.

3. Drain on food grade paper towels.

Plantains

Purchasing: Choose fruit that is firm. Can be green, it will just take time to ripen.

Serving: When unripe, the plantain is similar to a vegetable. When ripe, like a banana, but must be cooked. Use with soups, stews, yams, apples, sautéed and served with fish or roast chicken.

Cooking: Sauté peeled, sliced plantain in a skillet with a little olive oil or butter. May be baked in its skin (wash outside with soap and water first) at 350°F for about 45 minutes to an hour; or grilled 4 inches above coals for about 35 minutes.

Storing: A green plantain can take 2 weeks to ripen. Keep at room temperature. When nearly black, and not ready to cook, they will keep another day in the refrigerator. You can also freeze ripe fruits. Peel first, wrap securely in wax paper.

Nutritional info: Like bananas, high in potassium, Vitamin C, Vitamin B6, magnesium and folic acid.

Asparagus Pudding

SERVES 6

This old-time Danish recipe is surprisingly tasty and good for you.

3 tablespoons unsalted butter	½ teaspoon salt
¼ cup all-purpose flour	½ teaspoon freshly cracked pepper
1 cup whole milk	1 pound fresh asparagus, trimmed and
¼ cup evaporated milk	finely chopped (canned is fine also)
6 large eggs, separated	

1. Melt butter in medium saucepan over moderate heat. Sprinkle in flour, stirring constantly to make a roux. Cook for 1 minute, until thickened, and golden. Gradually whisk in milk. Cook for 2 minutes. Remove from heat and cool for 10 minutes. Preheat oven to 350° F. Grease an 8 by 8-inch glass baking dish. Set aside

2. Beat egg yolks until frothy. Blend into milk mixture. Beat egg whites until stiff. Fold into egg yolk mixture.

3. Spoon half of egg mixture into baking dish. Top with asparagus, then remaining egg mixture. Bake until golden and puffy, about 35 minutes.

Okra Rice

MAKES 6 SERVINGS

1 small onion, minced	2 cups okra diced
1 clove garlic, crushed	½ teaspoon salt
1 stalk celery, minced	½ teaspoon dried thyme
1 tablespoon olive oil	½ teaspoon freshly cracked black
1 cup rice	pepper
2 cups water	

1. Sauté onion, garlic and celery in olive oil in a medium saucepan over moderate heat until vegetables are soft, about 3 to 4 minutes.

2. Add water and bring to a boil. Stir in rice, okra, salt, thyme and pepper. Bring to boil again, reduce heat, cover and cook until all water is absorbed by rice. Cooking time varies with type of rice used. See rice package directions.

Rice and Pigeon Peas

SERVES 4 TO 6

You can find pigeon peas in the canned section of your grocery store. Substitute any small bean, lentils included.

1½ teaspoons sea salt (coarse is best)
6 whole peppercorns
3 garlic cloves, crushed
1 small onion, minced
3 culantro leaves, or ¼ cup freshly shredded cilantro
½ cup freshly shredded parsley
1 tablespoon freshly shredded thyme, or 1 teaspoon dried
¼ cup olive oil

1 red bell pepper, seeded and sliced in ¼ inch strips
1 strip bacon (cooked) ham hock, or pig tail (optional)
½ teaspoon thyme
¼ teaspoon marjoram
1 bay leaf
1 cup white or brown rice
1 15-ounce can pigeon peas, drained
2 cups water

1. Using a mortar and pestle, pound together salt and peppercorns until pulverized. You can also use a small electric coffee mill. Transfer pepper mixture to food processor along with garlic, onion, cilantro, parsley, thyme and olive oil. Process until smooth.

2. Sauté pepper mixture along with red bell pepper in a large saucepan over moderate heat for 6 minutes. Crumble in bacon, stir, and cook 1 minute. Add marjoram, thyme, bay leaf, rice and water. Bring to boil, reduce heat, cover and cook until all water is absorbed from rice. Just before all water is absorbed, fold in drained pigeon peas, and fluff.

Norman Island

The most southernly of all the British Virgin Islands, Norman Island lies across Flanagan Passage from the U.S. Virgin Island of St. John. It has a huge bay on the north shore between Water Point and Treasure Point. Rumor has it the caves at Treasure Point conceal pirate treasure. Norman Island may possibly have been the inspiration for Robert Louis Stevenson's novel *Treasure Island*.

Chutneys, Hot Sauce and Seasonings

Mango-Ginger Chutney

MAKES ABOUT 32 OUNCES

This good and basic chutney goes with just about anything. Keeps nicely in the refrigerator for weeks. Make extra to give as gifts.

½ teaspoon coriander	2/3 cup cider vinegar
½ teaspoon turmeric	3 cups slightly green mangoes, peeled, seeded and chopped
¼ teaspoon cardamom	
¼ teaspoon cinnamon	1 medium onion, minced
¼ teaspoon nutmeg	½ cup raisins
¼ teaspoon allspice	1 small dried red hot pepper, minced
¼ teaspoon cloves	2 garlic cloves, crushed
1¼ cups white sugar	2 tablespoons freshly grated ginger

1. Toast spices in a small dry skillet for 1 minute over medium heat until slightly darkened and a fragrant aroma released. Remove from heat and set aside.

2. Bring sugar and vinegar to a boil in a large heavy saucepan. Add mango, onion, raisins, pepper, garlic and ginger. Return to boil, reduce heat and simmer for 30 minutes, until mixture has slightly thickened.

3. Pour into sterilized canning jars with rubber rings. Seal jars and plunge into boiling water. Boil for 15 minutes, and then carefully remove jars from hot water with canning tongs. Cool, then refrigerate. Will keep up to 8 weeks unopened.

Peter Island

This pristine jewel is located about five miles across the Sir Francis Drake Passage from Road Town, Tortola. You can take your own boat or a ferry. The entire island is owned by Peter Island Resort, which includes 50 luxury rooms, two restaurants, a gift shop, and ample water sports. The beaches are fantastic, in particular Deadman's Bay.

Hot Sauce

MAKES ABOUT 1 CUP

Use more or less peppers to taste. You can also use a milder pepper if you like.

1 large onion, minced
3 cloves garlic, crushed
  juice of two limes
1 green bell pepper, minced
1 red bell pepper, minced

3 small habañero peppers, seeded and minced
¼ cup vegetable oil
¼ cup vinegar

1. Toss onions and garlic with lime juice. Set aside in a non-reactive (glass or ceramic) bowl at room temperature for 2 hours.

2. Scoop onion mixture into a large skillet. Add peppers and vegetable oil. Sauté over medium heat, bring to a boil, reduce heat, cover and simmer for 20 minutes. Remove from heat and stir in vinegar.

3. Cool and store in sterilized glass bottles. Keeps up to one month in the refrigerator.

Banana Catsup

MAKES ABOUT 3 CUPS

I know the recipe sounds strange, but it's wonderful alongside any main course entrée or rice dish.

2/3 cup golden raisins
1 medium yellow onion, minced
2 garlic cloves, crushed
½ small jalapeño pepper, or other spicy pepper
¼ cup tomato paste
½ cup apple cider vinegar
2 tablespoons olive oil
5 large ripe bananas, peeled and cut in chunks
¼ cup fresh lime or lemon juice
3 cups water

½ cup packed brown sugar
½ teaspoon cinnamon
½ teaspoon allspice
¼ teaspoon cardamom
1/8 teaspoon nutmeg
½ teaspoon salt
½ teaspoon freshly grated black pepper
1 teaspoon freshly grated lemon or lime rind

1. Puree raisins, onion, garlic, pepper, tomato paste and olive oil in a food processor until smooth.

2. Add bananas, lime juice, water, sugar, spices, salt, pepper and lemon rind, processing until smooth.

3. Pour into a medium saucepan and bring to a boil over medium heat. Reduce heat, cover and simmer for 1 hour. Remove from heat and cool.

4. Strain through a sieve and transfer to a sterilized jar. Keeps in refrigerator for about a month because of the acid in the vinegar and the lime juice.

The William Thornton

The William Thornton restaurant is located on an old Baltic trader ship anchored off Norman Island. I'm embarrassed to admit in all my years in the Virgin Islands, I have never been to the William Thornton. My ex-husband had a boat, and we often traveled to Peter Island, Virgin Gorda, and Jost Van Dyke, but he never took me there. Perhaps because of the rumors-guests, under the influence of rum, dove naked off the ship, and I guess he didn't want me doing that.

Curried Banana and Green Mango Chutney

MAKES ABOUT 1 ½ QUARTS

Serve with curries, fish, chicken and meat dishes.

2	tablespoons olive oil	1	cup apple cider vinegar
1	medium onion, minced	¼	cup lemon juice
1	tablespoon freshly grated ginger	½	cup orange juice
2	cloves garlic, crushed	1	cup brown sugar
½	small jalapeño or habañero pepper, minced	1	teaspoon curry powder
		1	teaspoon freshly grated orange peel
2	large unripe mangos, peeled and cut in ½-inch cubes	½	cup raisins
4	large, slightly green bananas, peeled and diced	½	cup toasted cashews, coarsely chopped

1. Sauté onion, ginger, garlic and pepper in olive oil in a large sauce pan over medium heat for 5 minutes until vegetables are soft. Add mango, banana, vinegar, lemon juice, orange juice, sugar and curry powder.

2. Bring to a boil, reduce heat, cover and cook for 15 minutes. Stir in orange peel, raisins and cashews. Remove from heat and allow to sit for ½ hour.

3. Pour into sterilized jars. Keeps in refrigerator for up to two weeks.

Stewed Guavaberry Sauce

MAKES ABOUT 3 TO 4 CUPS

Guavaberries can be a bit hard to come by on the U.S. mainland. Substitute whole cranberries. I prefer light brown sugar over dark, which can impart a heavy caramel taste.

1 pound guavaberries (washed and seeds removed) or whole cranberries	1 pound light brown sugar
1 stick cinnamon	1 pound granulated sugar
1 clove	3¼ cups water

1. Combine all ingredients in a deep saucepan or stockpot. Bring to a boil, stir, reduce heat, and simmer, uncovered for about 1 to 1 ½ hours until you have a jam-like consistency.

2. Remove from heat, and remove cinnamon stick and clove. Spoon into sterilized jars. Serve as a pastry filling, or as a side dish to curries and other spicy dishes.

Guava Cheese

MAKES ABOUT 24 1-½ INCH SQUARES

This recipe is more like a candy gummy bear or fruit roll up than a cheese. Guavas are native to tropical America and are related to cinnamon, nutmeg and clove. The fruit is about 2 to 3 inches in size, its flesh anywhere from white, yellow or salmon. Very fragrant, slightly sour taste.

4 pounds ripe guava	2 sticks cinnamon
3 cups granulated sugar	¼ teaspoon ground cardamom
1½ cups water	1 teaspoon grated lemon rind

1. Wash guavas and peel. Place in a large pot with 1 ½ cups water and the sugar. Bring to a boil over moderate heat, reduce heat, cover and simmer for 45 minutes, stirring now and then. Cool. Puree in food processor until smooth.

2. Return to saucepan along with cinnamon, cardamom and lemon rind. Bring to a boil, reduce heat and cook until mixture leaves the side of the pot. Drop a ½ teaspoonful into cool water. It should form a firm ball.

3. Grease a shallow dish and pour guava mixture in, removing cinnamon sticks. Cool and cut in squares.

Achiote Citrus Marinade

MAKES ABOUT 1 ½ CUPS

Achiote seeds are prized in Caribbean cuisine because of their slightly bitter, earthly flavor and iodine red color. You can purchase in Hispanic section of grocery stores or order online. Use on poultry, fish or meat dishes like a barbeque paste.

¼ cup achiote seeds
½ cup orange juice
¼ cup fresh lemon or lime juice
¼ cup olive oil
1 small onion, minced

½ small habañero pepper, seeded and minced
1 garlic clove, crushed
½ cup shredded cilantro or culantro
½ teaspoon salt

1. Grind achiote seeds in a small coffee bean mill.

2. Combine achiote powder, orange juice, lime juice, olive oil, onion, garlic, pepper, cilantro, salt and black pepper in a food processor until smooth.

Avocado Relish

SERVES 4

Serve as dip with tortilla chips, on salad or on the side with main course entrees.

2	large ripe avocados	½	teaspoon salt
3	tablespoons fresh lemon or lime juice	½	teaspoon cayenne pepper
1	medium ripe tomato	½	teaspoon freshly cracked black pepper
1	small onion, minced		
1	clove garlic, crushed		
½	small habañero pepper, seeded and minced		

1. Peel avocado, discard seed and chop in ½-inch pieces. Sprinkle with lemon juice. Set aside.

2. Chop tomato. Combine with onion, garlic, pepper, salt, cayenne and black pepper. Fold into avocado. Toss gently.

Cooper Island

This small, hilly island is about eight miles from Road Town, Tortola, and quite popular with the charter boat crowd. There is only one hotel on the island, which has 12 charming, no-frills units. The sole restaurant on the island offers delicious island fare such as conch fritters and chicken roti. Excellent diving.

Island Barbeque Rub

MAKES A LITTLE OVER ¼ CUP

Quite similar to a 'jerk' rub. Keep on hand to make short, tasty work of last minute meals. Good for chicken, fish or pork.

2	tablespoons salt	1	teaspoon onion powder
2	tablespoons freshly cracked black pepper	1	teaspoon ground allspice
		1	teaspoon ground cumin
2	tablespoons parsley flakes	1	teaspoon cayenne pepper
2	tablespoons brown sugar	1	teaspoon paprika
1	teaspoon garlic powder	¼	teaspoon cinnamon

Combine all ingredients in a small bowl. Transfer to a jar with a tightly fitting cover.

Cakes, Breads and Desserts

Baked Coconut Dumb Bread

MAKES 2 LOAVES, 4 TO 6 SERVINGS

You can find this wonderful sweet bread in bakeries all over the U.S. and British Virgin Islands. Delicious with tea or coffee in the morning. I've adapted this recipe to be more flaky, not dry and crumbly.

2	cups all-purpose flour		1	cup unsweetened grated coconut
2	teaspoons baking powder		¾	cup unsweetened coconut milk
3	tablespoons sugar		¼	cup evaporated milk
½	teaspoon salt		2	tablespoons water
¼	cup vegetable shortening			
2	tablespoons butter, room temperature, but still cool			

1. Sift together flour, baking powder, sugar and salt. Cut in vegetable shortening and butter until mixture resembles crumbly sand. Work in grated coconut.

2. Slowly add coconut milk, milk and water. Knead for 10 minutes until a smooth elastic bowl forms. Cover and rest for 20 minutes.

3. Preheat oven to 350° F and grease a cookie sheet.

4. Cut dough in two and roll out on a heavily floured surface. Form into two flattish loaves. Bake for 20 to 25 minutes until golden and a toothpick inserted in center comes out clean.

Benye

MAKES 24

Benyes are similar to New Orleans beignets, except they have bananas and spices added. Very nice for breakfast with strong coffee or tea.

1	package instant yeast		¼	teaspoon nutmeg
1	cup warm water		¾	cup sugar
4	cups all-purpose flour		1½	teaspoons grated orange peel
½	teaspoon cinnamon		2	tablespoons melted butter
½	teaspoon cardamom		2	large ripe bananas mashed
½	teaspoon clove			vegetable oil for frying
¼	teaspoon mace			

1. Dissolve yeast in warm water. Set aside

2. Sift together all dry ingredients in a large bowl. Stir in warm water and yeast, stirring vigorously for 2 minutes. Add orange peel, butter and

mashed bananas until well combined. Cover and keep in a warm spot for 2 hours.

3.   Heat 1-inch of vegetable oil to 360° F. Drop batter by spoonfuls into hot oil. Fry until golden. Drain on food-grade white paper towels.

Ducana

MAKES 24 DUMPLINGS

Ducana is a sweet potato dumpling that often accompanies salt fish and other fish dishes.

1 cup unsweetened grated coconut (fresh if you have it)	2 cups all-purpose flour
2½ cups peeled sweet potato, grated by a food processor	½ cup finely ground cornmeal
1 teaspoon vanilla	¼ cup finely ground raw almond (almond meal)
½ teaspoon almond extract	½ cup sweetened condensed milk
1 tablespoon melted butter	½ cup water

1.   Combine coconut and sweet potato in a large bowl. Stir in vanilla and almond extract and butter. Set aside.

2.   Stir flour, cornmeal and raw almond meal together in a large bowl. Fold in coconut/sweet potato. Combine condensed milk and water in a small bowl. Stir into flour mixture. You should have a firm dough.

3.   Fill a large pot with slightly salted water. Bring to a boil over medium heat.

4.   Place by the heaping tablespoon full in foil pouches, folding over and securing ends. Lower pouches into simmering water. Boil for 30 to 35 minutes. Remove with tongs and drain. Unwrap and serve along fish and other main dishes.

Sweet Bread

MAKES 12 SERVINGS

Traditionally Virgin Islanders served Sweet Bread with sliced ham during the Christmas holiday season. Plan on soaking the dried fruits in brandy or rum by Thanksgiving or earlier. My husband's grandmother started after Labor Day.

1	cup golden raisins	4	cups all-purpose flour
1	cup currants	1	teaspoon salt
1	cup pitted prune, coarsely chopped	1	teaspoon cinnamon
¼	cup freshly grated orange peel	½	teaspoon nutmeg
3/4	cup dates, coarsely chopped	½	teaspoon cardamom
2	cups brandy or rum	¼	teaspoon allspice
2	packages yeast	½	cup whole milk
2	cups butter	½	cup evaporated milk
2	cups light brown sugar	1	cup coarsely chopped walnuts
8	eggs		

GLAZE

½	cup brandy or rum	½	cup sugar
		1	teaspoon almond extract

1. Soak raisins, currants, prunes, dates and orange peel in the brandy at least 4 weeks prior to making bread.

2. Dissolve yeast according to instructions on package. Set aside.

3. Cream together butter and brown sugar until light, about 10 minutes. Beat eggs until frothy, and whisk into butter, beating for additional 10 minutes. Stir in almond extract.

4. Sift together all dry ingredients, except nuts, and beat into butter/egg mixture. Stir in milks, beating until smooth. Fold in yeast water, soaked fruit and nuts. Cover and keep in a warm place for 4 to 5 hours.

5. Preheat oven to 350° F. Grease a tube or Bundt pan and dust generously with flour. Spoon batter into pan. Bake 1 ½ hours until a toothpick inserted in center comes out clean. Cool on a wire rack for 15 minutes, then invert on a cake plate.

6. Prepare glaze by boiling ½ cup sugar with the ½ cup brandy for 10 minutes until slightly thickened. Remove from heat and stir in almond extract. Drizzle over top of cake.

Black Cake

MAKES UP TO 36 SERVINGS

I got into this cake one year when I was pregnant with my daughter Roxanne. This is a fruit cake which has been soaked in Guavaberry Liqueur or Cherry Brandy for up to a month before serving. This cake's rich, concentrated flavor improves with time.

1 cup pitted prunes, snipped in half, or quarters if large	1 cup granulated sugar
1 10-ounce package dried figs, chopped	4 large eggs
1 cup raisins	2 teaspoons vanilla extract
1 cup dried apricots, chopped	2¼ cups flour
1 cup dried dates, chopped	2 teaspoons baking powder
1 cup candied cherries	½ teaspoon baking soda
1½ cups chopped walnuts	1 teaspoon salt
1 cup butter, softened	1 to 1½ cups guavaberry liqueur or cherry brandy

1. Combine prunes, figs, raisins, apricots, dates, cherries and walnuts in a large bowl. Set aside.

2. Cream together butter and sugar until just blended (set mixer on low). Beat on high for 2 minutes until light and fluffy. Beat in eggs one at a time along with vanilla. Set aside.

3. Preheat oven to 325° F. Grease 10-inch tube pan, lining bottom with parchment-grease parchment.

4. Sift together flour, baking powder, soda and salt. Gradually beat into wet ingredients. Fold in fruit and nuts. Spoon into prepared pan. Bake for 1½ hours until toothpick comes out clean. Cool in pan on a wire rack. While hot, poke holes in cake with a skewer. Pour ½ cup of brandy over top.

5. Wet a knife and run around edge of pan to loosen cake from pan. Remove parchment. Wrap in foil or plastic wrap and refrigerate overnight. Remove from refrigerator, place in plastic or tin cake holder. Refrigerate, sprinkling with additional brandy every couple days. Keeps up to 4 weeks in refrigerator.

Pineapple Courting Cake

SERVES 8 TO 10

This tropical treat, originally made with strawberries, came from the northern part of England. Young girls made this for their betrotheds.

1 cup butter	1½ cups heavy whipping cream
¾ cup fine sugar	2 tablespoons Amaretto™ or almond liqueur
3 large eggs, lightly beaten	1 cup fresh or canned, diced pineapple, drained
2 cups all-purpose flour	
1 teaspoon baking powder	
½ cup evaporated milk	

1. Preheat oven to 375°F. Lightly grease three, 9-inch round baking pans and line bottoms with parchment (greasing that as well).

2. Cream and butter and sugar together using an electric hand mixer set on high until almost white, about 5 minutes. Beat in one egg at a time.

3. Sift together flour and baking powder. Beat into butter mixture 1/3 at a time, alternating with milk. Divide batter equally between three pans. Bake for 12 minutes, then rotate top and bottom pans to ensure even cooking. Remove pans from oven and cool on wire rack.

4. Beat whipped cream until stiff peaks form. Whisk in Amaretto™. Turn out cakes. Cover one cake with 1/3 of the whipped cream and 1/3 of the pineapple. Repeat with second layer. Cover top of cake with whipped cream, and dot decoratively with pineapple.

Mango Tart with Coconut Meringue

MAKES 6 SERVINGS

pre-baked tart shells
3 large ripe mangos, peeled and chopped
½ cup packed brown sugar
1 cup heavy cream
juice of two limes
1 tablespoon lime zest

4 egg whites
½ teaspoon cream of tartar
¼ cup sugar
½ cup toasted sweetened, grated coconut

1. Combine mangos and brown sugar in a small saucepan. Bring to a boil, reduce heat and simmer for 10 minutes. Remove from heat.

2. Beat heavy cream with lime juice and zest for 5 minutes until thick. Set aside

3. Beat egg whites, 1/4 cup sugar and cream of tartar with an electric mixer until stiff peaks form. Fold in toasted coconut.

4. Preheat oven to 350° F. Scoop cooled mango filling into tart shells. Spoon lime cream on top. Divide meringue topping evenly between tarts.

5. Bake for 20 minutes until meringue is golden.

Trés Leches Cake

SERVES 8 TO 10

1½ cups all-purpose flour	½ teaspoon freshly grated lemon zest
1 teaspoon baking powder	1 cup whole milk
½ cup unsalted butter	¾ cup evaporated milk
1¾ cups sugar	¾ cup sweetened condensed milk
¼ cup lightly packed brown sugar	¼ cup Amaretto or almond liqueur
6 large eggs, lightly beaten	1¼ cups heavy or whipping cream
2 teaspoons vanilla	

1. Preheat oven to 350°F. Grease and flour a 9 x 12-inch baking pan.

2. Sift together flour and baking powder in a medium bowl. Cream butter, ¾ cup sugar and ¼ cup brown sugar until almost white in a separate bowl. Stir in eggs to butter mixture. Fold butter/egg mixture into flour mixture until smooth along with vanilla and lemon zest, but not over beaten or cake will fall. Pour batter into prepared pan. Bake for thirty minutes or until a cake tester inserted in center comes out clean. Cool for thirty minutes.

3. Combine whole milk, evaporated milk, condensed milk and almond liqueur in a large measuring cup. Prick top of cake in a dozen places with a fork. Pour milk mixture over top of cake. Refrigerate for several hours or overnight.

4. Whip cream until soft peaks form. Gradually beat in remaining cup of sugar until stiff. Spoon over top of cake.

Whipped Papaya with Rum and Lime

MAKES 4 SERVINGS

2 cups ripe papaya pulp	4 egg whites, beaten until stiff
¼ cup lime juice	1 cup heavy or whipping cream
2 teaspoons freshly grated lime zest	2 tablespoons sugar
¼ cup sugar	2 tablespoons rum
¼ cup lightly packed brown sugar	

1. Combine papaya, lime juice, zest and sugars in a food processor until smooth.

2. Fold in beaten egg whties until just incorporated. Spoon into glass serving bowl or trifle dish.

3. Whip cream until light peaks form. Gradually beat in sugar and rum. Spoon over papaya.

Coconut Custard

SERVES 6

1 cup grated coconut (unsweetened and fresh is best)
½ cup unsweetened coconut milk
1 can evaporated milk
1 can sweetened condensed milk

½ teaspoon cinnamon
¼ teaspoon cardamom
5 eggs
½ cup sugar

1. Combine grated coconut, coconut milk, evaporated milk and condensed milk in a medium bowl. Beat in cinnamon, cardamom and eggs with an electric mixer for 5 minutes until frothy. Set aside. Preheat oven to 325° F.

2. Sprinkle sugar on the bottom of a ceramic or glass oven-proof dish. Heat on top of stove until sugar caramelizes. Remove from heat.

3. Pour custard mixture on top over caramel. Set dish inside another dish filled with 1-inch of water. Bake for 45 to 60 minutes until custard is set.

Piña Colada Cheesecake

SERVES 12

COCONUT CRUST:
2 cups plain breadcrumbs
½ teaspoon ground cinnamon
1 cup flaked sweetened coconut

¼ cup ground almonds
½ cup butter, melted
1 teaspoon vanilla extract
9 or 10-inch spring-form pan

FILLING:
2 pounds cream cheese, room temperature
¾ cup sugar
½ cup cream of coconut (the sweetened kind used to make Piña Coladas, not coconut milk)

4 large eggs, room temperature
1 teaspoon Key lime or Persian lime zest
¼ cup heavy cream
3 tablespoons evaporated milk (unsweetened)
3 tablespoons sour cream

TOPPING:
   20-ounce can crushed pineapple
4 tablespoons brown sugar

1 tablespoon cornstarch (or use agar-agar found at the health food store)
1/3 cup rum

1. CRUST: Adjust oven rack to middle position. Preheat oven to 325°F. Line bottom of spring-form pan with foil, wrapping extra foil beneath pan. Assemble pan.

2. Combine breadcrumbs, ground almonds, cinnamon, coconut, butter and vanilla in a small bowl. Press onto bottom and sides of pan. Bake for 10 minutes and set aside to cool.

3. FILLING: Beat cream cheese with an electric mixer until fluffy. Slowly add sugar and beat until sugar is dissolved, about 3 minutes. Incorporate

cream of coconut. Add eggs 1 at time, until just mixed in, and then add the next. Scrape down bowl sides after each egg. Stir in zest, heavy cream, evaporated milk and sour cream.

4. Pour filling into prepared pan. Bake fifty-five minutes at 325°F, until sides pull away from pan, but center jiggles. Shut off oven, and using the handle of a wooden spoon to hold door ajar, keep in oven for an additional hour.

5. Remove from oven and set on wire rack to cool. Once at room temperature, refrigerate until chilled, 3 to 4 hours. Keeps for several days in the refrigerator.

6. TOPPING: Heat the crushed pineapple, juice and all, sugar, and cornstarch in a saucepan over low heat, stirring constantly until boiling. Reduce heat, simmer until mixture thickens. Cool for 20 minutes and stir in rum. Cool in refrigerator and spoon over top of cheesecake.

Drunken Bread and Butter Pudding

SERVES 8 TO 10

5 tablespoons butter, room temperature	¼ cup packed light brown sugar
½ loaf French bread, or other crusty bread, thinly sliced	4 eggs lightly beaten
	1 cup evaporated milk
	1 cup whole milk
½ cup raisins	½ teaspoon cinnamon
1 tablespoon freshly grated lemon or grapefruit zest	¼ teaspoon cardamom
	¼ to ½ cup rum

1. Lightly butter the bottom of an oven-proof dish. Butter bread, then place ½ the slices on the bottom of the dish.

2. Top with raisins, lemon zest, and half the sugar. Top with remaining bread slices.

3. Beat together eggs and milks, along with cinnamon and cardamom. Pour over bread, to with remaining sugar.

4. Preheat oven to 325°F. Allow bread to soak up egg mixture. Bake for 40 minutes until golden on top and custard is jiggly.

5. Remove from oven and drizzle rum over top. Serve hot, with ice cream or whipped cream.

Ginger Island

Ginger Island is uninhabited but popular because of the deep wall dive to Alice in Wonderland on South Bay. The dive site gets its name from the mushroom-shaped corals.

Chocolate Rum Cake

SERVES 12

I receive many email requests for rum cake recipes. The following is one of the quickest and best recipes I've come across.

chocolate baking powder (Hershey's)

1	package chocolate cake mix
1	package instant chocolate pudding mix
5	eggs, beaten
½	cup vegetable oil
½	cup water
¼	cup rum
1	cup semi-sweet chocolate bits
½	cup 151-proof rum

FROSTING:

½	cup butter, room temperature
2/3	cup chocolate baking powder (Hershey's)
1	teaspoon instant coffee (decaf is fine)
2¾	cup powdered sugar
1/3	cup evaporated milk
1	teaspoon vanilla

1. Preheat oven to 325° F. Grease a Bundt pan and dust with cocoa powder.

2. Beat together cake mix, pudding mix, eggs, oil, water and rum for 2 minutes on high speed. Do not over beat as cake will fall apart. Fold in chocolate bits. Spoon into prepared pan.

3. Bake for 55 to 60 minutes. Remove from oven and cool on wire rack for 10 minutes. Poke holes into cake randomly. Pour 151-rum over top while still warm. Invert cake onto cake plate and allow to cool before frosting.

4. FOR FROSTING: Beat cocoa powder and instant coffee into butter using an electric mixer on high speed. Whisk in powdered sugar, milk and vanilla.

5. Spread frosting over top and sides of cake.

Chocolate Rum Trifle

SERVES 8

4	egg yolks, lightly beaten
¼	cup extra-fine sugar
2	tablespoons Hershey's™ cocoa powder
1¾	cups whole milk
1	teaspoon vanilla extract
¼	cup rum

2	cups heavy whipping cream
¼	teaspoon ground cinnamon
24	lady finger sponges
2	cups mango or peach preserves
2	cups cubed fresh mango, juice reserved

1. Beat egg yolks, sugar and cocoa powder until light and fluffy. Bring milk to a boil in a medium saucepan. Reduce heat to low, and slowly whisk in eggs and vanilla extract. Stir until mixture thickens to a custard. Stir in rum and remove from heat.

2. Whip cream with cinnamon until stiff peaks form. Fold into custard. Set aside.

3. Cut lady fingers in half, and spread with mango preserves. Arrange a layer of lady fingers in bottom of bowl. Moisten with reserved mango juice. Top with chocolate cream and layer of mangos. Repeat until all lady fingers, cream and mango is used up. Chill for several hours before serving.

Chocolate-Coconut Rum Balls

MAKES ABOUT 36

If you don't like coconut, substitute grated white or plain chocolate to roll the balls in.

¾ cup heavy whipping cream	1 tablespoon Kahlua™ or coffee liqueur
12 oz. good quality, semi-sweet chocolate bits	3 tablespoons butter, room temperature
2 tablespoons Hershey's™ cocoa powder, sifted	1 16-ouce package of Hershey's Kisses™
¼ cup rum	1 cup sweetened grated coconut

1. Bring heavy cream in a small saucepan to a boil over medium heat. Remove from heat and stir in chocolate until melted. Whisk in cocoa powder, rum, Kahlua and butter. Stick in freezer for 15 to 20 minutes until firm enough to roll into balls.

2. Using a melon baller, scoop up chocolate and place on a waxed sheet. Chill in refrigerator until firm.

3. Melt Hershey's Kisses™ slowly in the top of a double boiler. Dip rum balls in melted chocolate, and roll in grated coconut or chocolate when slightly cooled. Store in refrigerator, not freezer.

Coconut Squares

MAKES ABOUT 12

You'll find these colorful coconut treat in local groceries and bakeries.

2 pounds granulated sugar	2 teaspoon vanilla extract, divided
1 cup whole milk, divided	1 teaspoons almond extract
¼ cup evaporated milk, divided	1 teaspoon orange extract
10 oz. unsweetened, grated coconut red and green food coloring	vegetable oil

1. Lightly oil two, 8-inch square glass baking dishes.

2. Melt sugar and ½ cup of the whole milk and 4 tablespoons of evaporated milk in a medium saucepan over moderate heat until sugar is dissolved. Turn up heat and bring to a boil, for about 10 minutes (soft ball stage, 240°F). Remove from heat and fold in half of coconut, one teaspoon of vanilla, almond extract and a few drops of red food coloring. Press into one of the oiled baking dishes.

3. Repeat with remaining ingredients, only using orange extract and green food coloring. Allow to set. Candy should break into pieces.

Non-Alcoholic and Alcoholic Tropical Drinks
Non-alcoholic drinks
Hibiscus Ale

MAKES 3 QUARTS

You can purchase dried hibiscus flowers from a number of herbal suppliers on line. Buy the whole organic flowers, not powdered.

1 cup dried hibiscus flowers	½ cup fresh lime juice
2 tablespoons grated ginger	1 teaspoon freshly grated lime zest
½ cup granulated sugar	¼ teaspoon almond extract
12 cups filtered water	

1. Bring hibiscus ginger, sugar and water to boil in a large saucepan. Remove from heat, cover and allow to steep for 2 hours.

2. Stir in lime juice, zest and almond extract when cool. Chill in refrigerator. Serve over crushed ice.

Ginger Beer

MAKES OVER 2 QUARTS

I love West Indian ginger beer. It doesn't even resemble ginger ale. It's spicy and sweet. Perfect over ice.

2 quarts filtered water	½ cup fresh lime juice
½ pound fresh ginger root, grated	1 tablespoon freshly grated lime zest
½ cup granulated sugar	¼ cup honey

1. Bring water, ginger and sugar to a boil in a large saucepan. Reduce heat, cover and simmer for 15 minutes. Remove from heat and cool.

2. Stir in lime juice, zest and honey. Refrigerate for 2 days. Serve over ice.

Maubi

MAKES 1 GALLON

Every day scientists discover new health benefits for herbs and seasonings. Rosemary and orange peel are potent anti-oxidants. Drink up to your health!

1 gallon of water	3 cinnamon sticks
1 large sprig of rosemary, or 2 small	2 tablespoons orange peel
3 sprigs sweet marjoram	½ teaspoon grated nutmeg
1 tablespoon anise seeds	2 cups sugar
6 small pieces of maubi bark	1 small yeast cake

1. Bring water to a boil. Add rosemary, marjoram, anise, maubi, cinnamon, orange peel and nutmeg. Reduce heat and simmer for 15 minutes. Add sugar and simmer additional 5 minutes.

2. Remove from heat when it foams, and cool. Strain into sterilized glass jars. Break up yeast cake and stir into mixture while still warm. Allow to stand overnight. After a while you'll see bubble rising. Keeps up to a week refrigerated. May contain some alcohol.

Sorrel

MAKES 2 QUARTS

1	pound sorrel	1	cinnamon stick
3	tablespoons grated ginger	½	teaspoon whole allspice berries
2	quarts water	2	cups sugar
4	cloves		

1. Rinse sorrel leaves and place in a large pot along with ginger, water, cloves, cinnamon, allspice and sugar. Bring to a boil. Remove from heat, cover and allow to steep overnight.

2. Strain and pour into sterilized glass jar. Keeps up to a week in the refrigerator.

Sea Moss

MAKES 1 ½ QUARTS

Sea Moss is a type of seaweed. All seaweeds are highly therapeutic and chock full of iodine, minerals and much needed amino acids.

1	pound of sea moss, or seaweed of choice	2	cups water
½	cup lime juice	¾	cup sugar
1	cinnamon stick	1	quart whole or skim milk

1. Soak seaweed overnight in lime juice. Bring to boil along with cinnamon stick, water and sugar. Reduce heat and simmer for 20 minutes until seaweed is gelatinous. Remove from heat and cool.

2. Remove cinnamon stick and puree in blender along with milk until smooth. Keeps for three days in refrigerator.

Little Thatch Island

When money is no object, this is the private island to be pampered at. Cost is $8,000 plus a day for 1 to 4 guests. Four, octagonal cottages have broad verandas, and three of the four cottages have outdoor, stonework showers. Complete with gourmet chef and staff which see to all your desires.

Alcoholic Tropical Cocktails

Banana Punch

MAKES 1 ½ QUARTS

2 ripe bananas, peeled and chopped
1 quart whole or skim milk
½ teaspoon vanilla extract
¼ teaspoon cinnamon

3 tablespoon honey
1 cup crushed ice
ground nutmeg

Whirl all ingredients in blender until smooth. Sprinkle with nutmeg.

Yo, ho, ho and a bottle of rum...

Caribbean rum had its beginning in Barbados in 1640, and rum distillation quickly spread throughout the islands. By the 1670's, rum was produced in the 1670's, and by the end of the century, more than 275 rum plants existed in the islands. Rum figured prominently as a tradable commodity, and became an integral part in the Triangle Trade, where slaves from Africa were exchanged for rum, which in turn was sold in Europe to raise more money to buy slaves.

Banana Daiquiri

MAKES 1 SERVINGS

2 ounces light or gold rum
½ ounce Crème de Banana liqueur
splash of Rose's lime juice

1 ripe banana, peeled
1 cup crushed ice
splash of milk or cream

Combine all ingredients in blender until smooth. Pour into a tall glass.

Bushwacker

MAKES 1 SERVINGS

1 ounce dark rum
1 ounce Bailey's Irish Cream Liqueur
½ ounce dark Crème de Cacao
½ ounce Kahlua

splash of Amaretto
grated nutmeg
½ cup crushed ice

Combine all ingredients in blender except nutmeg until smooth. Pour into a tall glass and garnish sparingly with grated nutmeg.

Guavaberry Liqueur

MAKES 2 ½ LITERS

The name 'guavaberry' is of Carib Indian origin. Guavaberries blossom directly on the branches without stems and have small pink and white flowers. The fruits are about ½-inch in size and are red or yellow. The fruit ripens after Thanksgiving, which is why it is associated with the Christmas holidays. If you can't find guavaberries, substitute cranberries with an equal amount of black cherries and blueberries.

3	pounds guavaberries	2	vanilla bean pods (expensive but worth it)
3	cups brown sugar		
1	cup water	½	teaspoon cloves
1	cup white sugar	1	cardamom pod (or ½ teaspoon powdered)
1	cup pitted prunes		
1	cup raisins	2	cups fresh or dried sorrel
2	sticks cinnamon	2	bottles of Cruzan rum

1. Rinse guavaberries and squeeze out seeds. Bring ½ of the berries to a boil along with sugar, water, prunes, raisins, cinnamon, vanilla, cloves, cardamom and sorrel. Reduce heat and simmer for 45 minutes until thickened. Stir now and then. Remove from heat and cool for 30 minutes.

2. Pour syrup into a sterilized glass jar or wide-mouth bottle. Add remaining uncooked berries and rum.

3. Store in a cool dark place for several months, shaking bottle once a week. The taste improves with age. Strain and serve neat, or over ice. Good for fruitcake recipes.

Grog

MAKES 1 SERVING

Admiral Sir Edward Vernon, returning from the Caribbean in 1740, was nicknamed "Old Grog" because his overcoat was made from a coarse fabric called grogram. The good Admiral thought his men drank too much rum, so he watered it down to improve work output. Lemon and lime juice was added later to help prevent scurvy.

2	oz. dark rum		barely a pinch, less than a ¼ teaspoon, ground cloves
6	oz. water		
1	tablespoon lime or lemon juice		pinch of nutmeg
1	tablespoon dark brown sugar	1	cinnamon stick

Gently heat all ingredients, except cinnamon stick and nutmeg, in a small saucepan until sugar disappears. Garnish with cinnamon stick and nutmeg.

Mango Magarita

SERVES 1

2 ounces tequila	splash of Triple Sec liqueur
2 ounces fresh or frozen mango chunks	½ cup crushed ice
2 ounces fresh lime juice	

Wet the rim of a large margarita glass with water. Twist in a dish of salt. Set aside. Whirl all ingredients in a blender until smooth. Pour into prepared margarita glass.

Mudslide

SERVES 1

1 ounce Stoli Vanil (vanilla) vodka	½ ounce Bailey's Irish Crème Liqueur
½ ounce Tia Maria or Kahlua	cola

Fill a rocks glass with ice. Stir in first 3 ingredients. Fill to top with cola. Garnish with an orange twist. Be sure to twist rind over drink for that precious drop of orange oil.

Painkiller

SERVES 1

1 ounce Pusser's British Navy rum	½ ounce Coco Lopez
1 ounce Pusser's 151 proof rum	ice chunks
2 ounces pineapple juice	freshly grated nutmeg
2 ounces orange juice	

Fill a rocks glass with ice. Stir in all ingredients except nutmeg. Sprinkle nutmeg over top.

Strawberry-Mango Daiquiri

SERVES 1

2 ounces rum	½ cup ripe mango chunks
½ ounce Framboise or strawberry liqueur	splash of Coco Lopez
	splash of heavy cream
½ cup frozen strawberries	1 cup crushed ice

Whirl all ingredients in blender. Pour into a tall glass.

Rum Cream Liqueur

ENOUGH FOR 4, MAYBE

It's really simple to make your own Bailey's™-style cream liqueur. Even in the islands, this type of liqueur is costly. You can substitute whiskey for the rum if you prefer.

¼ cup light brown sugar, packed	¼ cup Drambuie™
3 tablespoons boiling water	2 cups light cream
1 teaspoon vanilla extract	1 teaspoon cocoa powder
½ cup dark or light rum	

Dissolve sugar in the boiling water. Cool. Stir in vanilla, rum, Drambuie™ and cream. Chill several hours before serving. Top with cocoa powder. Keeps several days in refrigerator.

Tortola Coffee

MAKES 1 SERVING

1 oz. rum	extra strong hot coffee or espresso
splash of Drambuie™	whipped cream
1½ teaspoons dark brown sugar	

Fill a coffee cup with boiling water, then pour out and wipe dry. Add rum, Drambuie™, sugar and hot coffee. Stir until sugar is dissolved. Top with whipped cream. Serve at once.

Zombie

MAKES 1 SERVING

This is my signature drink!

1 ounce light rum	½ ounce grenadine syrup
1 ounce dark rum	crushed ice
2 ounces pineapple juice	orange slice
1 ounce orange juice	½ ounce 151 proof rum
1 ounce fresh lime or lemon juice	

Whirl all ingredients, except 151-proof rum and orange slice, in a blender until smooth. Pour into a tall glass. Float 151 on top, garnish with orange slice.

Glossary of Caribbean Foods

Allspice: Also known as pimento or Jamaican pepper, it is used in jerk seasoning. The berries resemble large peppercorns, and taste like cinnamon, nutmeg, and clove.

Annatto: Annatto are red seeds and are also called achiote. The Carib Indians used these seeds prior to Columbus' arrival to the new world. They add a bright red color to food, and are high in Vitamin A.

Arrowroot: A white starch used as a thickening agent in cakes, soups and gravies.

Bammie: A round flat bread made from cassava.

Breadfruit: A large green fruit with rough skin the size of a bowling ball. When roasted resembles baked potato.

Calabaza: West Indian pumpkin, orange flesh, sweeter than pumpkin, high in Vitamin A.

Callaloo: A vegetable which resembles spinach; used in a stew called Callaloo that contains shellfish and is traditionally served during Christmas holidays.

Cassava: A long tuberous root vegetable, with rough dark skin. Arawak and Carib Indians squeezed the poisonous juice out to make delicious cassava bread.

Cayenne: A hot peppery powder made from an assortment of seeds and pods of pepper plants, reddish brown in color.

Chayote: Type of squash, pear-shaped and light green in color.

Christophene: See chayote.

Chili powder: Ground chili pepper usually containing other spices such as cumin, oregano and salt.

Cinnamon: Made from the bark of the cinnamon tree.

Cloves: Have a delicious aroma and are the buds of Eugenia aromatic, a type of tropical tree.

Coconut: A large seed of the coconut palm, up to 100 feet tall. Grows well in salt air and in sand, hence they line up on beaches. The inside is edible and used in cakes, curries and pies. To make coconut milk, put water in a blender, and slowly add fresh coconut pieces until a milk-like consistency is attained.

Coriander: Leafy herb used in curries.

Cumin: An herb with a flavor similar to caraway, also used in curries.

Curry: Herb and spice mixture which may contain any or all: turmeric, coriander, cumin, chili, fennel, fenugreek, cardamom, clove, cinnamon, nutmeg, black pepper.

Custard apple: Similar to soursop, but smaller. Flesh is creamy white, with custard-like texture, large black seeds, sweet and tart.

Dasheen: Another tuber common to the West Indies, large round with rough brown skin like tree bark, used in soups and stews.

Ginger: Aromatic tuberous rhizome used in curries, chutney, and desserts.

Guava: Small 3 to 4 inch fruit, with small hard seeds, sweet and aromatic.

Jerk: Highly seasoned paste used to flavor meat, chicken and seafood. Contains chili peppers, onions, allspice, garlic, ginger, thyme, nutmeg, cinnamon and lime juice.

Johnnycake: Fried bread-like fritters made from water, salt, flour and baking powder.

Kiwi: Egg-sized oval fruit with fuzzy brown skin and lime green flesh. Tastes like a cross between a strawberry and banana.

Mango: The queen of Caribbean fruits, fragrant, juicy, resembling intense peach.

Okra: Finger-length green pods used in vegetables and stews.

Papaya: Also known as paw-paw, can be eaten ripe or green, used for jams, drinks, and salads.

Paprika: Shockingly bright red powder made from mild chili peppers.

Passionfruit: Fruit the size of a golf ball with thick, brownish purple skin growing on a vine. Flowers are magnificent. Flavor resembles pineapple, lemon and guava, used for drinks, desserts, salads.

Plantain: Similar to a banana, but must be cooked. May be eaten green or ripe, boiled or fried. High in protein, potassium, iron, calcium and some B vitamins.

Soursop: see custard apple.

Starfruit: Also called carambola, yellowish, the size of a pear grown on trees. When cut cross-wise resembles a star, taste like pear, apple and melon.

Sweet potato: Often confused with yams, sweet potato is a tuberous vegetable, orange or white. High in Vitamin A and C.

Tamarind: Tart juicy fruit that is brown and pod-like. Use to make jams and candies when ripe; when unripe for chutneys and curries. Tamarind is used in Angostura Bitters and Worcestershire.

Taro: see dasheen

Turmeric: A type of ginger, bright yellow in color. Good antioxidant.

Yam: Can weigh up to 20 pounds, tuberous root vegetable, high in Vitamin A.

INDEX

Order Blank
Books by Angela Spenceley

Shipping: Continental U.S. Add $4.00 1st item, add $3.00 each subsequent item. International and Canada: $15.00 1st item, $10.00 each subsequent item. Please make check or money order payable to: Coconut Press, LLC, P.O. Box 79710, Carolina, PR 00984-9710 website: www.coconut-press.com

	Quantity	Price	Total
A Taste of Florida, The Keys and Caribbean	_____	$14.99	_____
A Taste of the Caribbean Cookbook, pp.292 Over 250 traditional and novelle recipes	_____	$19.99	_____
A Taste of the Virgin Islands Cookbook pp.32	_____	$8.99	_____
A Taste of Puerto Rico Cookbook pp. 32	_____	$8.99	_____
A Taste of the British Virgin Islands	_____	$8.99	_____
A Taste of St. Croix	_____	$8.99	_____
A Taste of Puerto Rico, Too! approx. 400 pp.	_____	$19.99	_____
Don't Drink the Water-Complete Caribbean	_____		_____
Bartending Guide	_____	$19.99	_____
Just Add Rum! Cookbook and drink guide pp 120	_____	$12.99	_____
How to Have Your Own Caribbean Luau 96 pp	_____	$9.99	_____
My Tiny Virgin Island Cookbook approx. 48 pp Other Caribbean books	_____	$5.99	_____
Guide to the U.S. Virgin Islands, English or Spanish 96 pages of color photos	_____	$18.99	_____
Guide to Puerto Rico, English or Spanish 96 pages of color photos	_____	$18.99	_____
Guide to the British Virgin Islands 96 pages of color photos	_____	$18.99	_____
Flowers of the Caribbean, 64 stunning pages	_____	$17.99	_____

Name:..

Address:...

City:.............................State:......................Zip: ....

email address:...

Notes

Notes

Notes

Notes